Ro-C4

ERIC KRESSNIG · CASE STUDIES

CASE

ERIC KRESSNIG

RITTER VERLAG

VORWORT

Eric Kressnig

Die Grundidee des vorliegenden Buches ist es, die prozessuale Entwicklung meiner wichtigsten Werkblöcke seit 2003 darzustellen. Dabei werden auch jene Arbeiten berücksichtigt, welche entweder nur für eine Ausstellung existierten oder nicht mehr in der vollständigen Version als Arrangement verfügbar sind.

Die Wahl des Titels „Case Studies/Fallstudien" soll die Vielschichtigkeit meiner Arbeit verdeutlichen. Die Auswahl der Autorin und der Autoren nimmt auf dieses Arbeitsprinzip Rücksicht.
Ausgehend von einem konkreten Anlass und einer künstlerischen Fragestellung werden in einer aktiven, situationsbezogenen Auseinandersetzung, Lösungsmöglichkeiten gefunden und künstlerisch begründet.

PREFACE

Eric Kressnig

The basic idea of this publication is to present the development of my most important groups of works since 2003. I also included those pieces that only existed for one exhibition or are no longer completely available in the original arrangement.

The title I selected – "Case Studies/Fallstudien" – is supposed to highlight the many different layers of my work. The authors selected for the accompanying essays also reflect my working principle.
This book was motivated by a specific occasion and it is also guided by a particular theme. I have sought to actively develop artistic responses to different situations and contexts.

ERIC KRESSNIG
VORWORT
PREFACE   5

MATTHIAS BOECKL
ELEMENTARE ALPHABETE
ELEMENTARY ALPHABETS   9

ANNETTE SÜDBECK
DER RAUM ALS MATRIX
SPACE AS A MATRIX   37

JAN MOKRE
LANDKARTEN ZWISCHEN WISSENSCHAFT UND KUNST
MAPS BETWEEN SCIENCE AND ART   58

THOMAS BALLHAUSEN
GEFLECHT.
NETWORK.   78

MARTIN ENGLER
DIRTY MINIMAL
MALEREI ZWISCHEN KONZEPT UND INTUITION
PAINTING BETWEEN CONCEPT AND INTUITION   99

ELEMENTARE ALPHABETE
ÜBER ERIC KRESSNIG

Matthias Boeckl

Eric Kressnig verfolgt in seiner Arbeit einen konzeptuellen Ansatz, der oft mit Konkreter Kunst assoziiert wird. Dieser Vergleich mit ähnlichen künstlerischen Strategien zeigt nicht nur die Vielfalt einer „Fraktion" der zeitgenössischen Kunstproduktion, sondern macht besonders auch die individuellen Schattierungen jener Fragestellungen deutlich, mit denen sich der Künstler befasst. Beispielsweise zeigte eine Ausstellung mit dem sperrigen Titel „Realität und Abstraktion 2 – konkrete und reduktive Tendenzen ab 1980", die im Sommer 2012 im Kärntner Privatmuseum Liaunig stattfand, Eric Kressnigs Arbeit in jenem Milieu, dem sie zu entstammen scheint und in dem ihre subtilen Qualitäten besonders gut zur Geltung kommen. Man sah Pioniere der klassischen Moderne, viele international bekannte Größen der Konkreten Kunst und eine beeindruckende Zahl an Zeitgenossen aus Österreich. Die „Pioniere" waren durch Josef Albers, Sol LeWitt und Pierre Soulages vertreten und die „Stars" der internationalen Szene wurden von Imi Knoebel, Tony Cragg und Heinz Mack repräsentiert. Unter den Österreichern fand man – sofern regionale Zuordnungen in der aktuellen Kunstproduktion überhaupt Sinn machen – unter vielen anderen großen Künstlern auch Hildegard Joos, Helga Philipp, Heinz Gappmayr, Richard Kriesche, Heimo Zobernig, Karl Prantl, Hans Kupelwieser, Jakob Gasteiger, Brigitte Kowanz, Peter Kogler und Eva Schlegel.

In der Ausstellung wurden zwei große Leinwandbilder Kressnigs gegenüber zweier Arbeiten von Karl Hikade und neben einem Objekt von Michael Kienzer gezeigt. Dieser Kontext ist gut geeignet, Kressnigs Arbeit zu positionieren und ihre inhaltlichen Stoßrichtungen mit verwandten Strategien zu vergleichen. Es ist keine Kunst für oberflächliche Betrachter. Man muss sich in eine akribische, mitunter trotzdem ironische Arbeitsmethode einfühlen, die dem

ELEMENTARY ALPHABETS
ABOUT ERIC KRESSNIG

Matthias Boeckl

In his work Eric Kressnig has adopted a conceptual approach that is often associated with concrete art. This comparison with similar artistic strategies not only points to the diversity of a 'faction' in contemporary art production. It also sheds light on the various nuances of the issues the artist focuses on. For instance, an exhibition with the unwieldy title "Reality and Abstraction 2 – Concrete and Reductive Tendencies Since 1980", which took place at the Liaunig, a Carinthian private museum, in the summer of 2012, showed Eric Kressnig's work in the setting from which it seems to stem – and it is here that its subtle qualities become particularly noticeable. Here one could see pioneers of classical modernism, many internationally known big names of concrete art and an impressing number of contemporary artists from Austria. The 'pioneers' included Josef Albers, Sol LeWitt and Pierre Soulages and the 'stars' of the international scene Imi Knoebel, Tony Cragg and Heinz Mack. Among the Austrians one found – to the extent that regional references make any sense at all in recent art production – next to the many big artists also Hildegard Joos, Helga Philipp, Heinz Gappmayr, Richard Kriesche, Heimo Zobernig, Karl Prantl, Hans Kupelwieser, Jakob Gasteiger, Brigitte Kowanz, Peter Kogler and Eva Schlegel.

The exhibition featured two large canvases by Kressnig, which were hung across from two pieces by Karl Hikade and next to an object by Michael Kienzer. Kressnig's work was well positioned in this context, which proved useful for comparing the artist's thematic thrust with related strategies. It is not an art for the superficial beholder. You have to be able to understand and relate to a meticulous, sometimes still ironic working method, which requires a heightened perception

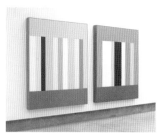

Untitled (Diptychon), 2011/2009
Acryl/Leinen, je 200 x 160 x 14 cm

Ausstellungsansicht: „Realität und Abstraktion 2 – konkrete und reduktive Tendenzen ab 1980", Museum Liaunig

Betrachter durchaus eine geschärfte Wahrnehmung abfordert. Dem schnellen, oberflächlichen Blick erschließt sich diese Kunst kaum. Kressnigs Formensprache ist durchgehend geometrisch. Das alleine sagt aber noch nicht viel aus, da ja – siehe oben – ein ganzer Kosmos konstruktiver Kunst existiert, der sehr verschiedenartige Fragestellungen thematisiert. Diese Sphäre der Kunstproduktion zeigt genau so viele verschiedene Stile und Techniken, ja sogar „Handschriften" wie die andere, die expressive, malerische, „realistische" Fraktion.

ELEMENTARE STRUKTUREN, IRRITATIONEN

Der Unterschied zwischen den beiden „Ausdrucksfamilien" liegt nicht in deren Begriff von Individualität und Authentizität, jenen Grundkategorien der Moderne, sondern in der Art des künstlerischen Empfindens. Es geht darum, welche Wahrnehmungen und Ereignisse den Künstler stimulieren und in eine Schwingung versetzen, die sich dann in der Kunstproduktion Bahn bricht. Für viele Künstler sind das etwa sinnliche Oberflächen und Körper von Menschen, Tieren oder Pflanzen. Für andere ist es etwa die Welt der Konsumobjekte, die sie zur Herstellung künstlerischer Metaphern und Modelle der Trash-Kultur stimulieren. Und wieder andere Künstler sind von der unendlichen Kombinatorik elementarster Zeichen, Formen und Materialien fasziniert, von den Möglichkeiten, aus diesen Zivilisations-Partikeln eine eigenständige, nahezu autonome künstlerische Welt zu konstruieren. Nahezu, denn all diesen Arbeiten wohnt stets noch ein sogenannter „Realitätsbezug" inne, da entweder die Provenienz der Formelemente oder der Kontext des Werks derartige Beziehungen zur Alltagswelt transportieren.

Kressnig ist natürlich dieser zuletzt beschriebenen Stimulanzien-Gruppe zuzuordnen. Bei ihm können es etwa bestimmte Materialeigenschaften sein, die seinen kreativen Assoziationsmotor in Gang setzen, oder auch räumliche Strukturen. Das klingt abstrakt, löst aber einen sehr konkreten Arbeitsprozess aus. Ein Beispiel: Für eine Installation im Museum moderner Kunst Kärnten wählte Kressnig den Grundriss des Hauses als Ausgangspunkt. Mit

from the viewer. To grasp this art more is needed than a hasty, superficial gaze. Kressnig's formal repertory is geometric through and through. Yet this alone does not say much, since – as we saw above – there is an entire cosmos of constructive art that addresses very different issues. Indeed this sphere of art production shows so many different styles and techniques, even 'signatures' as the other, expressive, painterly – 'realistic' – group.

ELEMENTARY STRUCTURES, IRRITATIONS

The difference between both "expressive families" lies not only in their notion of individuality and authenticity, those basic categories of modernism, but rather in the type of artistic sensitivity. The issue is which perceptions and events stimulate the artist and bring on an impulse, which then manifests itself in art production. For many artists, this can be the sensual surfaces and bodies of individuals, animals or plants. For others it can be the world of consumer objects that provide inspiration for the production of artistic metaphors and models of trash culture. And then there are other artists who are fascinated by the endless combinations of the most elementary signs, forms and materials, the possibilities of constructing a separate, almost autonomous artistic world out of these civilizational particles. And only almost, since inherent to almost all of these works is a so-called "reference to reality", since either the provenance of formal elements or the context of the work conveys such references to the everyday world.

The impulses described last could, of course, be associated with Kressnig. In his case, it could be certain material qualities that activate his creative motor of association or even spatial structures. This sounds abstract but it actually triggers off a very concrete working process. An example: For an installation at Carinthia's Museum of Modern Art Kressnig took the ground plan as his point of departure. He set about working with a pencil and a ruler, beginning with the white wall of

Untitled, 2007
Buntstift, Graphit
50 x 65 cm

Bleistift und Lineal machte er sich ans Werk. Zur Verfügung stand eine weiße Wand des Museums, über die er einen feinen Linienraster legte. In regelmäßigen Abständen trug er dann in etwas dickeren Strichen abstrahierte Varianten des Museumsgrundrisses in den Raster ein. Allerdings wurde nicht die gesamte Wand mit diesen Chiffren einer Blockrandbebauung mit Innenhof bedeckt, sondern nur eine Fläche in der Gestalt einer U- oder G-Form. Diese Großfigur, die aus der Summe der Varianten der Kleinform besteht, spielt ihrerseits wieder auf die Grundrissfigur des Museums an. Aus einer vorhandenen, aber nicht als Kunst wahrgenommenen Struktur wird also ein Formsystem destilliert und variiert, das sowohl mit der Alltagserfahrung zu tun hat (Darstellung des Baus) als auch eine weitgehend autonome Struktur zeigt – eine subtile Verklammerung verschiedener Realitätsebenen und -maßstäbe durch das Kunstwerk. Kressnig hat für diese durchgehende Interdependenz aller Kunst- und Realitätsebenen eine schöne Kurzbeschreibung gefunden: „Each completes the other and is completed by the other".

Es wäre aber ein Irrtum, würde man annehmen, dass damit eine hermetische Ordnung geschaffen wird, aus der es kein Entrinnen gibt. Im Gegenteil: Kressnig liebt die feine Irritation, ja stellt sich mitunter sogar absichtlich die Frage: „Wie breche ich ein System"? Natürlich geht es dabei um nichts Destruktives, nicht um die Zerstörung eines einmal gefundenen Formgesetzes, das ja eine unbestreitbare Faszination ausübt, sondern eben um eine subtile Irritation. Auch dafür gibt es Beispiele, etwa in einer Serie an Buntstiftzeichnungen, in denen einfache geometrische Formen den ersten Eindruck bestimmen. Es sind unregelmäßige Vierecke, Pfeilformen, Dreiecke und dergleichen. Sie sitzen in einem exakten Rahmen aus Bleistiftstrichen, den sie mit ihren Eckpunkten berühren. Auch ihr eigener Umriss ist mit präzisen Bleistiftlinien gezogen. Ihre Binnenfläche allerdings zeigt die erwähnten Irritationen. Sie ist als merkwürdig flirrende Textur aus parallelen, eng gesetzten Buntstiftlinien in verschiedenen Abständen und Farbtönen ausgeführt. Die Farbnuancen sind fein aufeinander abgestimmt – entweder es sind Gelb-braun-Töne oder Rot-blau-Klänge, die sich wie

the museum over which he placed a fine grid of lines. In regular intervals he added, in the somewhat thicker lines of the grid, abstract variants of the museum's floor plan. However, he did not cover the entire wall with these signs of a perimeter block development featuring an inner courtyard and only worked with a U- or G-shaped surface. This large figure composed of the sum total of all variants of the small form, alludes, in turn, to the ground plan structure of the museum. The artist distills and varies a formal system from an existing structure that is not perceived as art which has to do with everyday experience (representation of the building) and reflects the largely autonomous structure – a subtle fusion of various levels and scales of reality in the artwork. Kressnig has found a nice way to describe this pervasive interdependence of all levels of art and reality: "Each completes the other and is completed by the other."

It would, however, be wrong to assume that a hermetic order has been thus constructed – one from which there is no escape. Quite the contrary: Kressnig lives subtle irritations, and sometimes he even deliberately asks: "How can I disrupt a system?" Of course, this is nothing destructive, and it is not the destruction of a given formal law, which undoubtedly exerts a certain fascination. Rather, it is, as noted above, a subtle irritation. For this one could also cite some examples, like the series of colored pencil drawings, in which simple geometric shapes govern one's first impression. There are irregular squares, arrow forms, triangles and the like. They are situated in a precisely drawn frame consisting of pencil lines that come together in the corners. Even their own outline has been precisely drawn with a pencil. Their inner surface, however, shows the irritations mentioned before. These have been executed as a strangely whirring texture of parallel lines drawn close together with a colored pencil in various intervals and in various shades of color. The nuances have been finely coordinated – either there are shades of yellow-brown or sounds of red and blue, elegantly placed over the

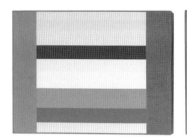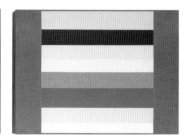

Neighbourhood
(Triptychon), 2009
Acryl/Leinen
je 70 x 90 x 13 cm

ein Teppich in einer enggewobenen Fadenstruktur elegant über das Blatt legen. Aber – darin besteht die Irritation – die farbigen Parallelstriche orientieren sich nicht an den Außenkanten der Drei- und Vierecke, sondern sind in einem minimalen Winkel leicht verschwenkt. So ergibt sich an der Innenseite der Umrisslinien eine gleichsam unklare Zone, in der die „Ordnung" des Bildes ins Rutschen gerät und sich die Schraffuren der Kante zwar annähern, aber sich nie mit ihr verbinden können.

WAS IST EIN BILD, WAS IST MALEREI?

Dieses Spiel mit Systemen, ihrer Ordnung und Irritation, mit Materialqualitäten und deren Umkehrung betreibt Kressnig in verschiedensten Techniken und Medien. Von der Zeichnung über die Druckgrafik und das Leinwandbild bis zu Objekten reicht das Medienportfolio des Künstlers. In der eingangs beschriebenen Ausstellung des Liaunig-Museums waren etwa zwei objekthafte Acrylbilder mit extrem tiefem Keilrahmen zu sehen. Statt der üblichen Stärke von wenigen Zentimetern sind Kressnigs Bilder 14 cm dick, was ihnen einen kastenartigen Charakter verleiht. Das ist der erste Schritt eines radikalen Antiillusionismus, der das Bild und die Malerei nicht als Abbild dieser oder einer anderen Welt interpretiert, sondern als ein autonomes Gebilde aus Material und Proportion, das seine eigenständige Gesetzmäßigkeit entwickelt. Die Elemente des so entstehenden Objekts werden säuberlich getrennt und vor dem Betrachter geordnet ausgebreitet. Der Bildträger ist das erste Element – eine nicht grundierte Naturleinwand, deren sinnliche Haptik durch die „Verdickung" auf eine fast ironische Art gesteigert wird. Auf diesem Bildträger liegt das zweite Element, nämlich das gemalte Bild – eine dünne Folie aus Farbe. Damit man diesen Foliencharakter noch besser erkennen kann, ist die bemalte Fläche freigestellt – links, oben und rechts bleibt ein sehr schmaler Streifen zwischen bemalter Fläche und Bildaußenkante frei, die Leinwand bleibt hier sichtbar (in den sorglosen Publikationen dieser Bilder fehlt dieser Rahmen). Am unteren Rand ist der unbemalte Streifen breiter, hier misst er fast ein Fünftel der Bildhöhe.

surface like a carpet with a tightly woven thread structure. Yet – and here's where the irritation lies! – the colored parallel lines are not oriented after the outer edges of the triangles and rectangles but have been slightly tilted at a minimum angle. Thus a sort of unclear zone emerges on the inner side of the contour lines – where the "order" of the picture begins to slip and the hatching moves towards the edge without being able to actually hook up with it.

WHAT IS A PICTURE? WHAT IS PAINTING?

Kressnig pursues this play with systems, their order and irritation, with material qualities and their inversion in a great variety of techniques and media. The artist's media portfolio ranges from drawing, print graphic and the canvas to objects. In the exhibition at the Liaunig Museum described at the beginning of this text there were two object-like acrylic paintings set in extremely deep wedge frames. Instead of the usual thickness of a few centimeters, theses paintings are 14 cm thick, which gives them a box-like look. This is the artist's first step towards a radical anti-illusionism, which does not interpret the painting as a depiction of this world or another one but rather reveals an autonomous entity of material and proportions, which develops its own regularities. The elements of the resulting object are painstakingly separated and then presented to the viewer in an orderly fashion. The picture surface is the first element – an unprimed natural canvas whose sensual haptic quality is enhanced in an almost ironic way by means of a "deeper" wedge frame. The second element lies on this surface, namely the painted picture – a thin layer of paint. To make it easier to recognize the quality of this layer, the painted surface is revealed – to the left, top and to the right a very narrow strip remains free between painted surface and the outer edge of the painting so that the canvas is visible here (in slapdash publications of these paintings this frame is left out.) On the lower edge the unpainted strip is broader, almost a fifth of the painting's height.

EK 011, 2011
Lithografie
je 65 x 51 cm

Was jedoch ist ein Bild, was ist Malerei? Malerei ist Komposition aus Farben und Formen, die in bestimmte Proportionen zueinander gebracht werden. Um das zu verdeutlichen, nimmt man am besten die einfachsten und klarsten Grundformen – Rechtecke. Wie die Formen müssen auch die Farben nahe an den Nullpunkt herangeführt werden – Kressnig verwendet dafür eine sehr schmale Palette aus Grau- und Blaugrün-Tönen. Das dritte Element der Malerei ist die Proportion. Und auch in dieser Kategorie zeigt Kressnig die grundsätzlichsten Lösungen: Die Boden- oder Horizontlinie ist ident mit der Grenze zwischen bemalten und nicht bemalten Partien der Leinwand. Die darauf stehenden Rechteckformen bilden in einem der beiden Bilder durch horizontale Aneinanderreihung ein Quadrat, womit das Grundprinzip der statischen Form dargestellt ist. Im zweiten Bild jedoch ziehen sich die Mann an Mann nebeneinander stehenden Rechtecke quasi „dynamisch" über die gesamte Bildbreite. Die Proportion dieses Feldes (~ 1,2) entspricht fast genau jener der Leinwand – gedreht um 90 Grad, womit angedeutet wird, dass es auch andersrum funktionieren würde. Tatsächlich hat Kressnig diese intelligente Bilderserie auch mit Horizontalstreifen weitergeführt. So kann man diese Leinwandbilder auch als Kommentar zu den Möglichkeiten von Bild und Malerei an sich lesen – man muss aber nicht. Man kann auch die eleganten Farbakkorde genießen, die exakte Konstruktion und den präzisen, ebenmäßig-dünnen Acrylfarbauftrag. Kressnigs Werke verfügen eben sowohl über eine intellektuelle als auch über eine sinnliche Ebene, sie sind beides – Aktion und Reflexion.

KUNST BUCHSTABIEREN

Die Arbeit mit Grundkategorien künstlerischer Produktion beschäftigt Kressnig auf allen Ebenen und in mehreren Maßstäben. Im Rahmen des Rudolf-Hradil-Grafikstipendiums in Salzburg befasste er sich auch mit der Lithografie. Dabei entstanden einige experimentelle Serien, die – wie zu erwarten – die Grundstrukturen des Mediums thematisieren. Dazu gehört etwa auch das

Yet what is a painting, what is painting in a more general sense? Painting is a composition of colors and shapes that can be related to each other in certain proportions. In order to visualize it is best to take the most basic and clearest shape – a square. Like shapes the colors also have to be brought close to the zero point – for this Kressnig uses a very limited palette of shades of gray and bluish-green. The third element of painting is proportion. And even in this category Kressnig offers the most fundamental solutions: The ground or horizontal line is identical with the boundary between painted and non-painted parts of the canvas. In one picture the rectangular shapes standing on it create a square through the horizontal sequence, thus offering a basic presentation of static form. However, in the second picture the rectangles that are lined up next to each other extend in a quasi 'dynamic' way over the entire picture. The proportion of this field (ca. 1.2) corresponds almost exactly to that of that of the canvas – tilted by 90 degrees, alluding to the fact that it could also work the other way around. Kressnig has actually continued this intelligent series of paintings with horizontal stripes as well. Thus these canvases can also be seen as a commentary on the possibilities of painting and the picture – but not necessarily. One can also enjoy the elegant accords of color, the precise construction and the meticulous, evenly thin layer of acrylic paint. Kressnig's works are endowed with both an intellectual and a sensual layer – they are both: action and reflection.

SPELLING ART

Kressnig is interested in working with the basic categories of artistic production on all levels and in a number of dimensions. While he was in Salzburg on a Rudolf Hradil graphic grant he also experimented with lithography. Here he created several series which, as was to be expected, addressed the basic structures of the medium. This also included format. In the history

EK 011, 2011
Lithografie/Hochdruck Buchdruck
je 65 x 51 cm

Format. In der Geschichte der Lithografie haben sich dazu einige Standards herausgebildet, etwa der „Basler Stab" – ein Stein von 37 x 49 cm. Kressnig „buch-stabiert" die Strukturen des Mediums, indem er monochrome Flächen in Pastelltönen druckt und darauf den maximalen Kontrast schwarzer Schrift setzt: Das Wort „Stab" erscheint dann mehrmals versetzt am Blatt. Oder es werden mehrere monochrome Flächen ohne weiteres Motiv versetzt übereinander gedruckt, was interessante Akkorde in Grau-grün-gelb-Klängen ergibt. Als Ortsbezug baute Kressnig wieder einen Grundriss ein – diesmal ist es die Salzburger Ursulinenkirche von Fischer von Erlach, deren markant dreieckiger Grundriss als abstrahiertes und durch mannigfache Reproduktion verdickt-verunklärtes Motiv alleine am Blatt steht. Für die Abschlussausstellung seines Studienaufenthalts druckte Kressnig Plakate, die konsequenterweise die grundlegendsten Irritationen thematisieren, derer das Medium – gedruckte Buchstaben – fähig ist. Beim Druck kann man sich verdrucken, sodass das Gedruckte etwa zweimal versetzt am Blatt erscheint – ein klassischer Fehldruck. Und bei der Schrift ist der fundamentalste Irrtum jener der verdrehten Stellung der Buchstaben. Kressnigs Plakate zeigen genau das – verdruckte und um 90 Grad verdrehte Schriftbilder, die lapidar den Inhalt kundtun und sonst nichts: „KRESSNIG IM TRAKLHAUS MON 5. DEZ 18.00".

Klar, dass ein Künstler mit dieser Interessenlage sich intensiv mit dem Phänomen des Buchstabens beschäftigt. Dieser minimalisierte Bedeutungsträger der kleinsten Einheit ist nicht nur wegen seiner sprachlich-semantischen Funktion faszinierend. Er ist auch Formgebilde. Und die Kombination einer „gegebenen" Form mit vielfältigsten Inhalten, zumal auf einer „molekularen" Ebene, ist natürlich eine einzige Herausforderung für Kressnig. Seine Antwort auf dieses Phänomen ist die Schablone, denn die einzelnen Sprachmoleküle werden ja in der alltäglichen Verwendung ident reproduziert. Sie können auch – um sie weiter zu vereinfachen – ihrer unregelmäßigen, kurvigen Elemente entkleidet und auf rechteckige Formen reduziert werden. Genau das tut Kressnig,

of lithography several standards have evolved, as for instance, the "Baslerstab" – a stone measuring 37 x 49 cm. Kressnig literally spells the structures of the medium by printing monochrome surfaces in pastel shades on top of which he has placed black type for maximum contrast. The word "Stab" (bar) appears several times on the sheet slightly off kilter. Or there are several monochrome surfaces without a further motif, printed on top of each other so they appear offset, which results in interesting accords in hues of gray-green-yellow. As a reference to a specific location Kressnig once again includes a ground plan – which this time is the Salzburg Ursuline Church by Fischer von Erlach, whose strikingly triangular ground plan stands alone on the sheet as an abstract motif, now thickened and blurred through the reproduction process. For the final exhibition of his study stay Kressnig printed posters that consistently address the most fundamental irritations which the medium – printed letters – is capable of. In the reproduction process they can be misprinted so that what is printed appears offset on the sheet – a classical misprint. And in the type the most fundamental error is that of the distorted position of the letters – Kressnig's posters show this precisely – letters that were misprinted and turned 90 degrees that only allude succinctly to the content and to nothing else: "KRESSNIG IM TRAKLHAUS MON 5. DEZ 18.00"

It is clear that an artist with these interests deals intensively with the phenomenon of type letters. This minimal signifier of the smallest unit is not just fascinating because of its linguistic-semantic function. It is also a formal element. And the combination of a 'given' form with a diversity of contents, especially in a 'molecular' level, is of course a big challenge for Kressnig. His answer to this phenomenon is the template as the individual linguistic molecules are reproduced identically in everyday use. They can also – to further simplify them- be stripped of their irregular, curved elements and reduced to rectangular shapes. This is precisely what Kressnig does, thereby creating a

Schriftfont, 2007
Größe variabel

schafft so eine eigene, gewissermaßen paradoxe Schrifttype: Indem sie das „Individuelle" der Schrift – Kurven, Serifen, Tropfen – eliminiert und durch die „neutrale" Geometrie ersetzt, schafft sie eine Kunst-Schrift, die aber klar einem Künstler als Erfindung zugeordnet werden kann. Das Subjektive wird so zum Objektiven und umgekehrt. Derlei Umkehrungen faszinieren Kressnig und er setzt sie konsequenterweise auch auf der formalen Ebene fort, indem er mithilfe seiner Schrift-Schablonen Bilder auf Leinwand malt. Die Buchstaben werden horizontal entlang der Mittelachse des Bildes angeordnet – schon diese erste Kompositionsentscheidung ist bereits auf Umkehrungseffekte angelegt, da sie eine horizontale Spiegelungsmöglichkeit suggeriert. Dazu kommt dann noch, dass die obere Bildhälfte in Grau und die untere in Weiß gehalten ist – und beim zweiten Bild umgekehrt. Dieser homogene Hintergrund wiederum erfordert, dass die darauf stehende Schrift je nach Bereich, auf dem ihre Teile stehen, invertiert werden muss, also die gegenteilige Farbe des Grundes hat, da sie ja sonst in diesem verschwinden würde. Das Ergebnis ist semantisch verwirrend, denn die Schrift ist kaum lesbar, aber die Struktur, die sich so ergibt, ist rhythmisch und schön. Also erneut eine paradoxe Umkehrung – durch formale Klärung und Reduktion wird semantische Unklarheit erzeugt, die sich aber auf ästhetischer Ebene wieder als Klarheit und Schönheit darstellt. Eine klassische philosophische Trias zwischen dem Material, dem Sublimen und dem Schönen. Zusätzlich zu diesen offensichtlichen Aspekten besitzen diese unscheinbaren Bilder auch noch eine Menge weniger auffälliger Eigenschaften, die die Lebendigkeit der Bilder betonen. So sind die Farbflächen nicht ganz homogen, das Grau ist nicht nur Grau, sondern auch gelblich, ebenso das Weiß. Die Bildkanten sind betont, indem wieder ein schmaler Rahmenstreifen angelegt wird, der in der jeweiligen Komplementärfarbe des betreffenden Bereichs gehalten ist. Und die Leinwände sind auch an den Seitenkanten bemalt, und zwar als „Fortsetzung" der Vorderseite in der Farbe des jeweiligen Rahmenbereichs.

separate type that is in a sense paradox. By eliminating the "individual" dimension of writing – italics, serifs, drops – and replacing it with "neutral" geometry, it creates a sort of art-writing which, however, was the artist's invention. The subjective thus becomes the objective and vice versa. Such inversions fascinate Kressnig and he continues them in a logical way on the formal level, by painting pictures on canvas using his type templates. The letters are arranged horizontally along the middle axis of the picture – already this first decision regarding composition is geared to creating inversion effects, since it suggests a horizontal reflection possibility. In addition, the upper half of the picture is gray and the lower is white – and in the second painting it is the opposite. This homogenous background in turn requires that the type, depending on the area in which its parts stand, must be inverted, that is have the opposite color of the ground since it would otherwise disappear in it. The result is semantically confusing, since the type is hardly legible, but the structure resulting from this is rhythmic and beautiful. So what we have is a new paradox inversion – semantic vagueness results from formal clarification and reduction but on an aesthetic level this vagueness manifests itself as clarity and beauty. It could be seen as representing a classical philosophical triad between the material, the sublime and the beautiful. In addition to these obvious aspects these unassuming pictures also have a number of less striking qualities that attest to the vibrancy of the artist's paintings. The color surfaces are not completely uniform – the gray is not just gray but also yellowish, just as the white is. The edges of the painting are underscored through a narrow strip on the frame, which is painted in the respective complimentary color of the given area. And the canvases are also painted on the side of the wedge frame – as a "continuation" of the front side in the color of the related section of the painting.

VOM GESCHLOSSENEN ZUM OFFENEN SYSTEM

Besonders anschaulich wird Kressnigs Methode in einer sehr unscheinbaren Zeichnungsserie, die bei einem Studienaufenthalt in Frankfurt entstand. Der Künstler bezeichnet sie als „offenes System aus 8 Blättern". Man sieht wenig, nur eine parallellogrammartige Form aus schwarzen Linien. Zwei horizontale Parallellinien oben und unten, dazwischen neun Schräglinien, die aber nicht alle die Horizontalseiten berühren: Beispielsweise sind in einem Blatt der Serie die Horizontallinien zu kurz, um sich noch mit den äußersten schrägen Vertikallinien links und rechts treffen zu können. Diese simplen Formen wirken auf den Betrachter derart bedeutungsfrei, dass man auf der Suche nach visuellen Reizen förmlich gezwungen ist, die sinnlich-haptische Struktur der Arbeiten genauer zu betrachten. Und so entdeckt man den unregelmäßigen Auftrag der Striche, ihre weich verlaufenden Enden, manche Verdickungen, mitunter sogar kleine Aussetzer. Irgendwie wirkt es aber nicht wie mit einem weichen Bleistift und dem Lineal gezogen. In der Tat: Es ist eine „mediatisierte" Zeichnung, da sie durch klassisches Kohle-Durchschlagpapier aufs Blatt gedrückt wurde. Dieses Durchdrücken ist wiederum kein zeichnerischer, sondern ein plastisch-skulpturaler Schöpfungsakt, weshalb Kressnig sagt: „Das ist mikroskopische Bildhauerei".

Die minimale Abweichung macht das geschlossene zum offenen System. Das ist eines der Grundelemente von Kressnigs Arbeitsweise. Es ist auch ein Symbol für Freiheit und unendliche künstlerische Imagination. Je klarer und strenger das System ist, desto dramatischer wirkt die Abweichung von ihm. In der eingangs beschriebenen Ausstellung in Kärnten 2012 wurde neben den beiden Bildern Kressnigs eine Arbeit von Michael Kienzer gezeigt. Eine Anzahl von Platten, wie sie die Industrie für den Innenausbau herstellt (Holzfaser, Pressspan, Glas etc.) liegt hier scheinbar beliebig übereinandergestapelt am Boden. An einer Seitenkante dieser rechteckigen Platten ist jeweils eine weitere Platte des gleichen Materials aufrecht stehend angeklebt, sodass sich eine Art skulpturales Raum-Eck aus ineinander gelegten Platten-Winkeln

FROM A CLOSED TO AN OPEN SYSTEM

Kressnig's method becomes particularly visible in a very unassuming series of drawings that the artist created while on a study trip in Frankfurt. The artist refers to it as an "open system of 8 sheets". Here one doesn't see much, only a parallelogram-like shape made of black lines. Two horizontal parallel lines on the top and bottom – in between there are nine slanted lines that, however, do not touch all of the horizontal sides. For instance, in one sheet of the series the horizontal lines are too short to be able to meet the outermost slanted vertical lines on the left-hand and right-hand side. These simple shapes strike the viewer as so bereft of meaning that while searching for visual stimuli one is literally forced to take a closer look at the sensual-haptic structure of the works. So this way one discovers the irregular application of the strokes, their soft ends, with some of the surface covered with thicker line and even some small surfaces left empty. But somehow it does not look as if they were drawn with a soft pencil and a ruler. Indeed, it is a "mediatized" drawing since it was pressed on paper with the classical transparent carbon paper. This imprint is in turn not a creative act of drawing but a sculptural one, which explains why Kressnig says: "This is microscopic sculpture."

The minimal deviation turns the closed system into an open one. This is one of the basic elements of Kressnig's approach. It is also a symbol for freedom and endless artistic imagination. The clearer and stricter the system is, the more dramatic the deviation from it seems to be. In the exhibition in Carinthia in 2012, described above, another piece, one by Michael Kienzer was also on display next to the two paintings by Kressnig. A number of boards, like those used industrially for interior construction (wood fiber, pressboard, glass, etc.) lie here, stacked in any odd way on the floor. On a side edge of these rectangular boards there is a further board made out of the same material standing upright, glued down, so that a sort of sculptural spatial corner is created with the angled wood joints, the board leaning

Offenes System, 2011
Carbon/Durex
29,7 x 21 cm

ergibt, das an der Wand lehnt. Das macht den Unterschied dieser Wandfigur zu einer Freiplastik aus, die frei im Raum stehen würde. Das leicht schräge Lehnen an der Wand ist aber auch ein technischer Widerspruch zur rechteckigen Verbindung der Platten. Denn wäre es tatsächlich ein rechter Winkel, würde das Objekt nicht an der Wand lehnen können und zur Freiplastik avancieren. Der Titel der Arbeit lautet daher auch „18 x 95 Grad", eben 95, nicht 90 Grad; Wandfigur, nicht Freiplastik. Auch Kressnig sucht derart Grenzgängerisches: Seine Leinwandbilder im gleichen Raum sind gleichzeitig Skulptur und Bild, ihre Komposition ist mal statisch, mal dynamisch. Ein künstlerisches System eben, das durch geringfügige Änderungen in Bewegung gerät und sich öffnet. Die Voraussetzung für die Entdeckung dieser Tatsachen ist Präzision, Konsequenz und Neugier. Klassische Künstler-Eigenschaften eben, die Kressnig in hohem Ausmaß besitzt.

on the wall. This is what makes this wall figure different from an outdoor sculpture, which would stand freely in a space. The slightly tilted leaning on the wall is, however, also a contradiction to the square connection of the boards. If it were really a right angle, the object would not be able to lean on the wall and become a freely standing sculpture. The title of the piece is thus "18 x 95 degrees". That is 95 degrees and not 90 degrees. A wall figure, not a freely standing sculpture. Kressnig is drawn to such tightrope walks. His canvases in the same space are both sculpture and painting, their composition is at once static and dynamic. That is to say, an artistic system, which begins to move through slight changes and opens up. The precondition for the discovery of these facts is precision, consistency and curiosity. Classical artist's qualities, which Kressnig certainly has no lack of.

S. 19, 21, 23, *Untitled*, 2008/11
Acryl/Leinen
200 x 160 x 14 cm

Offenes Stück, 2011
Acryl/Leinen
120 x 120 x 15 cm

Über Unter (Diptychon), 2010
Acryl/Leinen
100 x 200 x 8 cm

Dagegen und Damit (Diptychon), 2009
Acryl/Vinyl/Holz
60 x 60 x 2 cm

S. 30/31, *Untitled*, 6-teilig, 2010
Acryl/Leinen
360 x 540 x 16 cm

Untitled (Diptychon, Detail), 2012

S. 34/35, *Untitled* (Diptychon), 2012
Acryl/Leinen, 190 x 340 x 20 cm

DER RAUM ALS MATRIX

Annette Südbeck

Eric Kressnig äußert sich in verschiedenen künstlerischen Medien: Malerei, Objekte, Druckgrafik, Installationen und Zeichnungen auf der Wand und auf Papier stehen in seinem Werk gleichwertig nebeneinander. Gleichzeitig überträgt er häufig einen Teil der Gesetze und Darstellungsmittel von einem Medium in ein anderes, um durch die Grenzüberschreitungen zusätzliche Möglichkeiten und Qualitäten auszuloten. Den jeweiligen Arbeiten haftet das andere Medium hernach wie ein Adjektiv an: Seine Malerei ist auch architektonisch, die Skulpturen sind auch zeichenhaft und die Wandzeichnungen sind auch malerisch oder typografisch. Um mich seiner Methodik der Bildfindung und Strategie der Abstraktion anzunähern, möchte ich mich im Folgenden allerdings exemplarisch auf die Gruppe der Wandzeichnungen konzentrieren.

Nachdem Kressnig 2005 in der Galerie White 8 erstmals direkt auf die Wand gezeichnet hatte, entwickelte er im Jahr darauf mit „react view" in der Galerie splitter art seine auch für spätere Wandzeichnungen charakteristischen Bildideen. „react view" besteht aus zwei Arten sich überlagernder Bleistiftstriche: einem Netz aus feinen, fast flirrenden Linien und darauf stehenden kräftigeren Strichen. Letztere bilden eine gleichförmige Anordnung aus Rechtecken, die in ihrer Gesamtheit die monumentale Form des Buchstabens T darstellen und in ihrem Inneren verschiedene geometrische Formen aufweisen. Diese Binnenzeichnungen, die an Grundrisse erinnern und wie kleine Bilder im Bild funktionieren, sind ebenso kräftig gezeichnet wie die sie rahmenden Rechtecke. In der Betrachtung überzeugt die Wandzeichnung durch die Vielfalt in der Gleichförmigkeit und die Ausgewogenheit der verschiedenen Ebenen und aufeinander bezogenen Maßstäbe. Die Systematik, die sich hinter dem komplexen Bildaufbau verbirgt, ist unmittelbar spürbar, erschließt sich

SPACE AS A MATRIX

Annette Südbeck

Eric Kressnig employs various artistic media: painting, objects, graphic print, installations and drawings on walls and paper. They all have equal status as forms of artistic expression. At the same time he sometimes transfers the rules and representational means from one medium to another, exporting new possibilities and qualities by crossing its boundaries. The different medium added is then described in terms of an adjective: his painting is architectural, the sculptures drawing-like and the wall drawings are painterly or typographical. To explore his pictorial approach and his strategy of abstraction I would, however, like to focus on the example of his wall drawing series.

After drawing directly on the wall at the Galerie White for the first time in 2005, Kressnig proceeded in the following year to develop the pictorial ideas that were to become characteristic of his later wall drawings in his "react view" at the Galerie White 8. "react view" consists of two types of pencil lines that overlap: a network of fine, almost flimmering lines and on top of them stronger lines. The latter create a uniform arrangement of squares that taken together depict the monumental shape of the letter T, revealing various geometric shapes on the inside. These inner drawings that resemble floorplans, like small images within an image, are drawn with just as strong strokes as the rectangles framing them. When viewed the wall drawing is striking because of the diversity found in the uniformity and the harmonious balance of various levels and relating scales. The system that lies behind the complex pictorial composition is immediately tangible but it is only fully comprehensible when you reconstruct the

jedoch vollends erst im Nachvollziehen der Formfindung. Kressnig generiert zunächst ein Liniennetz, indem er den Raum, beispielsweise seine Höhe und Breite, die Abstände zwischen Fenstern oder jene zwischen Decke und Türöffnung, vermisst und mit diesen Proportionen die Abstände zwischen den Linien bestimmt. Das daraus resultierende Netz bildet in der Folge dann die Grundlage und das Maß für die Erfindung der Figuren. Diese sind dem Netz quasi immanent, werden aber erst durch das nochmalige Nachzeichnen von Linienabschnitten hervorgehoben und so förmlich aus diesem herausgezeichnet. Aus dem festgelegten, reduzierten Repertoire des Netzes wird dabei eine überraschend große Formenvielfalt erzeugt. Die strikte, selbstgewählte Systematik öffnet sich zu einem Spiel mit Auswahl- und Kombinationsmöglichkeiten.

Der Akt, direkt auf die Wand zu zeichnen, impliziert in den meisten Fällen eine intensive Auseinandersetzung mit dem Raum. Neben der Temporalität zählt insbesondere die Ortsbezogenheit zu den wesentlichen Darstellungsmitteln des Mediums Wandzeichnung. Durch die Wahl der Wand als Bildträger ist der Raum sowohl als physikalische Größe als auch als spezifische Situation in die Wandzeichnung eingebunden. Eine Wandzeichnung wiederum existiert nur in Verbindung mit dem Raum, ist materiell kaum davon zu lösen und wird meistens im Verbund mit diesem wahrgenommen. Wie also gestaltet Kressnig diesen Dialog? Um die Präsenz des Raumes und seine Funktion in den Wandzeichnungen genauer zu beleuchten, erweist sich der Begriff der Matrix als hilfreich. Dieser wird vielfach verwendet, um auf eine Anordnung in Form einer Tabelle zu verweisen. Aus dem Griechischen kommend bedeutet er wörtlich „Stamm, Muttertier", im übertragenen Sinn auch „Grund, Ursache". Die Matrix unterscheidet sich somit wesentlich vom Raster, das auf das lateinische *rastrum*, „Rechen, Hacken" zurückgeht und ein Liniengitter bezeichnet, das als standardisierendes oder ästhetisches Ordnungssystem über etwas gelegt wird. Das Raster bzw. Gitter spielt als Motiv in der Kunstgeschichte des 20. Jahrhunderts von Piet Mondrian über Agnes Martin bis hin zu Sol LeWitt eine bedeutende Rolle:

process of drawing. Kressnig first creates a network of lines by measuring the space, for instance, its height and width, the distances between windows or between ceiling and door opening, he then uses these proportions to define the distances between the lines. The resulting network subsequently produces the foundation, the scope for inventing the figures. These figures are in a sense immanent to the network but they only clearly emerge when the different sections of the lines are traced again, when they are literary drawn out of the network.
A surprisingly large diversity of forms is produced out of the defined, reduced repertory of the network. The strict, self-selected system opens up and gives way to a play with different possibilites of selection and combination.

The act of drawing directly on the wall usually involves an intensive preoccupation with the space. In addition to temporality, site-specificity is one of the crucial representational means of the medium of wall drawing. By selecting the wall as the picture support the space is integrated in the wall drawing both as a physical dimension and as specific situation. A wall drawing in turn only exists in conjunction with the space, it can hardly be detached from it in a material sense and is usually perceived in tandem with it. How does Kressnig go about structuring this dialogue? In order to gain a better understanding of the presence of space and its function in the wall drawings, the concept of the matrix proves useful. It is often used to refer to an arrangement in the form of a diagram. Derived from Greek it means literally, "dam, mother animal" and in a more figurative sense also "reason, source ". The matrix thus differs in a crucial sense from grid which goes back to the Latin word rastrum, "rake, hoe " and refers to a grid of lines that is placed of something as a standardizing or aesthetic system of classification. The raster or grid has played a significant role in 20th century art history from Piet Mondrin to Agnes Martin and on to Sol LeWitt:

Each completes the other and is completed by the other (Detail), 2011
Wandzeichnung, Buntstift, Graphit
420 x 620 cm

„Auf der räumlichen Ebene proklamiert das Raster die Autonomie der Kunst. Flach, geometrisch, geordnet, ist es anti-natürlich, anti-mimetisch, anti-real. So sieht Kunst aus, wenn sie der Natur den Rücken kehrt. Mit seiner durch die Koordinaten bedingten Flächigkeit verdrängt das Raster die Dimensionen des Realen und ersetzt sie durch die seitliche Ausbreitung einer einzigen Fläche. In seiner durchgängig regelmäßigen Organisation ist es nicht das Ergebnis von Nachahmung, sondern ästhetischen Dekretierens. Insofern seine Ordnung die reiner Beziehungen ist, spricht das Raster natürlichen Gegenständen den Anspruch auf eine eigene Ordnung ab. Das Raster zeigt, daß die Beziehungen im ästhetischen Feld in einer separaten Welt existieren und daß diese Beziehungen in bezug auf die natürlichen Gegenstände sowohl vorgängig als auch endgültig sind."[1]

Es ist eben diese Aufkündigung der außerbildlichen Gegenständlichkeit, die Kressnig in seinen Wandzeichnungen zurücknimmt, wenn er den Raum zur Matrix seiner Wandzeichnungen macht und von den spezifischen Gegebenheiten ausgeht, um sein Liniennetz zu entwickeln. Trägt er einerseits keine existierende Struktur in den Raum hinein, so sind seine Vermessungen des Raumes andererseits auch kein numerisches Resultat, das wie etwa die Wandzeichnungen von Mel Bochner aus den späten 1960er-Jahren darauf abzielt faktische Realitäten zu unterstreichen oder zu verdoppeln. Vielmehr verwendet er die vor Ort gefundenen Proportionen als Ausgangslage für neue, zahlreich variierte Bildfiguren.

Einschiebend möchte ich anmerken, dass der Raum sich auch noch auf einer anderen Ebene als Matrix der Wandzeichnungen verstehen lässt, denn als haptische Oberfläche beeinflusst die Wand in ihrer Materialität unmittelbar die Strichqualitäten. Ihre Unebenheiten und Risse zeichnen sich in den Linien ab und verändern deren Kontinuität und Farbdichte. Über die Wand als Zeichengrund wird der Raum also in doppelter Hinsicht zur Grundlage des Werkes.

"In the spatial sense, the grid states the autonomy of the realm of art. Flattened, geometricized, ordered, it is antinatural, antimimetic, antireal. It is what art looks like when it turns its back to nature. In the flatness that results from its coordinates, the grid is the means of crowding out the dimensions of the real and replacing them with the lateral result not of imitation, but of aesthetic decree. Insofar as its order is that of pure relationship, the grid is a way of abrogating the claims of natural objects to have an order particular to themselves; the relationships in the aesthetic field are shown by the grid to be in a world apart and, with respect to natural objects, to be both prior and final."[1]

It is precisely this break with external objectivity that Kressnig retracts in his wall drawings when he turns the space into the matrix of his wall drawings and proceeds from specific conditions to develop his network of lines. While he does not introduce any existing structure into the room, his measurings of the space are at the same time also not a numeric result which like Mel Bochner's wall drawings from the late 1960s are aimed at underscoring or doubling actual realities. Instead, he uses the proportions he finds on site as a basis for developing new pictorial figures that appear in numerous variations.

I would also like to note that the space can also be understood on a different level as a matrix of wall drawings, since as a haptic surface the materiality of the wall directly influences the line qualities. Their unevenness, the scissures are reflected in the lines, changing their continuity and the density of the color. Because the wall is the base of the drawing the space becomes the foundation of the work in a dual sense.

Die Figuren, die Kressnig aus dem Liniennetz entwickelt, lassen sich isoliert durchaus als autonome Figuren lesen, gleichzeitig wird die Verbindung zum ursprünglichen Bezugspunkt, zur Matrix des Raumes jedoch nie aufgegeben, bleibt das Liniennetz doch stets sichtbar. Diese doppelte Lesbarkeit erzeugt eine Art Kippmoment. Die Wandzeichnungen verbinden die außerbildliche Gegenständlichkeit des Raumes mit einer gewissen Selbstreferenzialität der daraus entwickelten Figuren, sie nehmen ihren Anfang in dem Einen, um auf das Andere hinzuarbeiten. Die Bewegung von der außerbildlichen Gegenständlichkeit zur Selbstreferenzialität, die nichts Geringeres als den Prozess der Abstraktion in seinem buchstäblichen Sinne von „Von-etwas-Abziehen" darstellt, wird von Kressnig durch die Übertragung der Motive in andere Medien weiter und teilweise bis zum Endpunkt getrieben. Die Radierung „react view – raster" beispielsweise zeigt einen Ausschnitt aus dem Liniennetz der gleichnamigen Wandzeichnung. Der Titel verweist präzise auf die nunmehr abgeschnittene Verbindung. Durch die Übertragung auf den transportablen Bildträger Papier fehlt dem Liniennetz seine ursprüngliche Grundlage, der Bezug zur Realität des Raumes. Es erscheint als autonomes Raster.

Vor diesem Hintergrund ist die Frage naheliegend, was mit den Wandzeichnungen geschieht, wenn ihnen der Raum abhanden kommt. Anders gefragt: Sind die Wandzeichnungen Kressnigs auf andere Räume übertragbar? Diese Frage mag auf den ersten Blick widersinnig erscheinen, gilt doch gerade die Ortsbezogenheit – wie schon oben behauptet – als eine der medialen Essenzen der Wandzeichnung. Ein Gegenbeispiel aus der jüngeren Kunstgeschichte, das eben diese Paradoxie auslotet, sind die Wandzeichnungen Sol LeWitts.[2] LeWitt trennte die Konzeption bzw. Idee einer Arbeit von ihrer materiellen Ausführung. Während seine sprachlich gefassten Konzepte unabhängig von den örtlichen Gegebenheiten sind, verdanken die jeweiligen Ausführungen ihren Charakter eben jener Spezifik. LeWitts Wandzeichnungen passen

The figures that Kressnig develops from the network of lines can certainly be interpreted in isolated form as autonomous figures. At the same time the link to the original reference point, to the spatial matrix is never given up, as the network of lines always remains visible. This dual legibility creates a sort of tilting effect. The wall drawings link the extra-pictorial objectivity of the space with a certain self-referentiality of the figures emerging from it. They assume their beginning in the one so as to work towards the other. The movement from extra-pictorial objectivity to self-referentiality, which represents nothing less than the process of abstraction in its literal sense of "abstracting something from something" is further pursued by Kressnig who transfers the motives into other media and in part to the final point. The etching "react view-raster", for instance, shows a section from the network of lines of the eponymous wall drawing. The title refers precisely to the now cut-off link. By being transferred to a transportable picture support the network of lines loses its original foundation, the reference to the reality of the space. It appears as autonomous.

Against this backdrop it might be natural to ask what happens with the wall drawings when they lose the space. Put differently: Can Kressnig's wall drawings be transferred to other spaces? At first glance this question might appear absurd, since site-specificity – as already said – is one of the essential qualities of the wall drawing medium. An alternative example taken from more recent art history which explores this paradox are the wall drawings by Sol LeWitt.[2] LeWitt separated the conception or idea of an artwork from its material execution. Whereas his linguistic concepts are independent of local condiitons, the individual realizations draw their character from this very specificity. However, LeWitt's wall drawings adapt to each real wall format through their abstract wording and can thus be repeated any time at other places. Kressnig's answer to the challenge sought, his

sich durch die Abstraktion in den Formulierungen jedem realen Wandformat an und sind dadurch jederzeit auch an anderen Orten wiederholbar. Kressnig's Antwort auf die gesuchte Herausforderung, seine Setzung der Konstanten und Variablen, ist eine andere: Bei der 2010 für die Firma Rutter Retail entstandenen Wandzeichnung löst er die Figuren aus ihrer räumlichen Verbindung, indem er stattdessen den Firmennamen des Auftragsgebers als Bezugsrahmen wählt. Die horizontalen und vertikalen Linienabstände der ersten Ebene des Netzes werden systematisch von den einzelnen Buchstaben abgeleitet, wobei der Abstand um so vieles größer ist, je weiter hinten im Alphabet der jeweilige Buchstabe steht. Die bildimmanente Relation zwischen dem Liniennetz und den Bildfiguren wird dadurch fest definiert, während ihre Beziehung zu den räumlichen Gegebenheiten offen bleibt, beziehungsweise wie bei der Hängung eines Gemäldes (immer wieder neu) vor Ort erfolgt. Was bleibt, sind das Spiel und die Dynamik der Formfindung auf der Grundlage einer Systematik, die einerseits willkürlichen Regeln folgt, andererseits doch einen nachvollziehbaren Ursprung hat. Dass Kressnig seine Bildfindungen verankert und sich dabei mit den Raumproportionen oder der Typografie eines Namens auf außerbildliche Gegenständlichkeiten und Artefakte bezieht, die bereits einen hohen Abstraktionsgrad besitzen, macht zu einem großen Teil die Spannung seiner Arbeiten aus.

placement of constants and variables is different. In the wall drawing created in 2010 for the company Rutter Retail he liberated the figures out of their spatial link by selecting the client's company name as the frame of reference. The horizontal and vertical line spaces of the first level of the network are systematically deduced from the inidvidual letters, with the space being by a factor larger than the corresponding letter behind it in the alphabet. The pictorially immanent relation between the network of lines and the figures is thus rigidly defined while their relation to the spatial gives remains open or as in the hanging of a painting is always set anew on site. What remains is the interplay and the dynamic of form evolving on the basis of a system that follows arbitrary rules on the one hand but on the other hand can also be tracked back to a clear origin. The tension of Kressnig's works derives largely from the fact that he anchors his pictorial creations while referring with his spatial proportions or typography to extra-pictorial objects and artefacts that already show a high degree of abstraction.

---

1 Rosalind E. Krauss, „Raster" (1979), in: Dies., *Die Originalität der Avantgarde und andere Mythen der Moderne*, hrsg. von Herta Wolf, Amsterdam, Dresden: Verlag der Kunst, 2000, S. 51f.

2 Vgl.: Annette Südbeck, *Eine andere Art zu zeichnen. Die Wandzeichnung bei Sol LeWitt, Hilka Nordhausen und David Tremlett*, München: Silke Schreiber, 2011.

1 Rosalind Krauss, "Grids" October 9, Summer 1979. [Reprinted in: *The Originality of the Avant-Garde and Other Modernist Myths.* Cambridge, MA: The MIT Press, 1985, pp. 9-22.

2 Cf.: Annette Südbeck, Eine andere Art zu zeichnen. *Die Wandzeichnung bei Sol LeWitt, Hilka Nordhausen und David Tremlett*, München: Silke Schreiber, 2011.

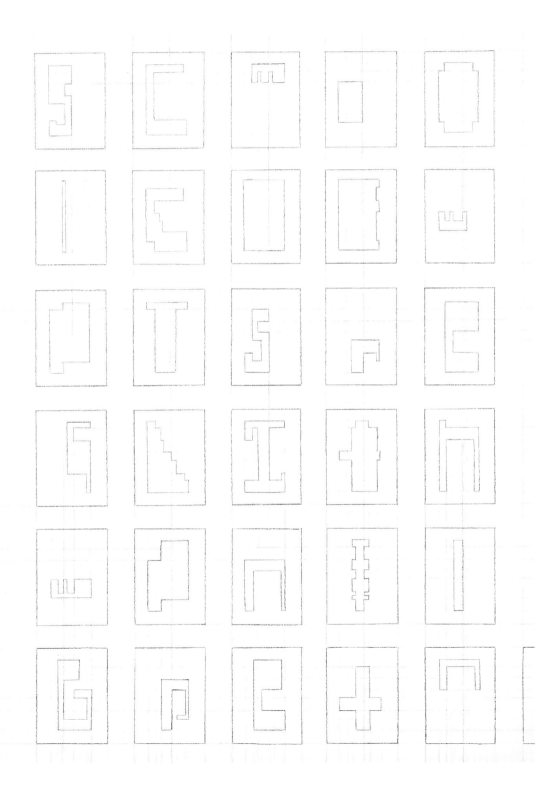

S. 42, Detail Wandzeichnung
S. 43, *Each completes the other and is completed by the other*
2011, Wandzeichnung, Buntstift/Graphit, 420 x 620 cm

S. 45, Modul, *Each completes the other and is completed by the other*
2011, Gesso/Graphit/4C Print/Papier, 28 x 20,5 cm

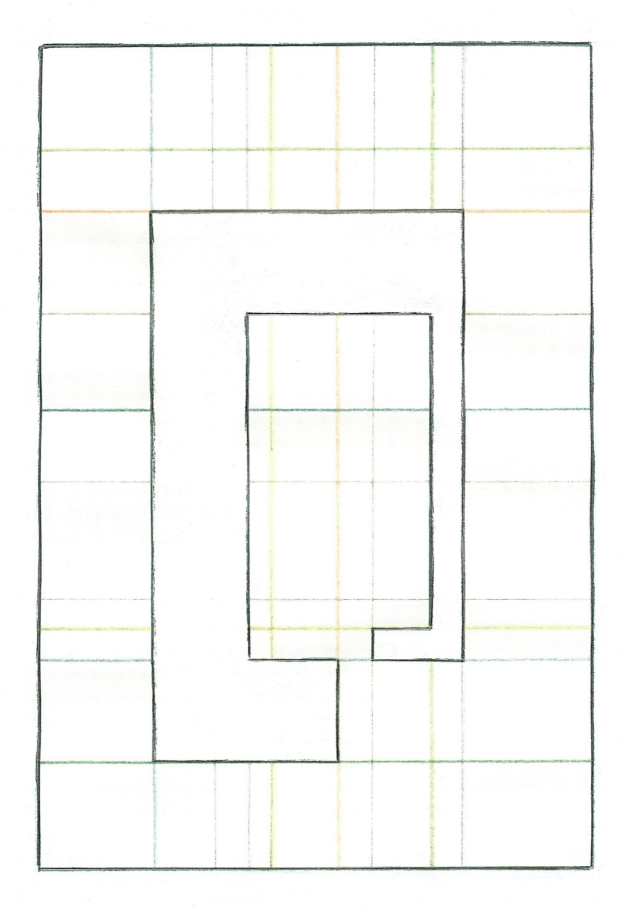

EVOL´R REVOL, 2009
Acryl/Vinyl/Holz
Ø 95 x 230 cm

LOVER	LEROV	LREOV	LVOER
LOVRE	LERVO	LREVO	LVORE
LORVE	LEORV	LRVEO	LVROE
LOREV	LEOVR	LRVOE	LVREO
LOEVR	LEVRO	LROVE	LVEOR
LOERV	LEVOR	LROEV	LVERO
OLVER	OERLV	ORELV	OVELR
OLVRE	OERVL	ORLEV	OVERL
OLRVE	OELRV	ORLVE	OVREL
OLREV	OELVR	ORLEV	OVRLE
OLEVR	OEVLR	ORVEL	OVLRE
OLERV	OEVRL	ORVLE	OVLER
VERLO	VOREL	VROLE	VLEOR
VEROL	VORLE	VROEL	VLERO
VELOR	VOELR	VREOL	VLOER
VELRO	VOERL	VRELO	VLORE
VEOLR	VOLER	VRLOE	VLROE
VEORL	VOLRE	VRLEO	VLREO
ELRVO	EROLV	EORLV	EVOLR
ELROV	EROVL	EORVL	EVORL
ELORV	ERLOV	EOVRL	EVROL
ELOVR	ERLVO	EOVLR	EVRLO
ELVRO	ERVOL	EOLRV	EVLOR
ELVOR	ERVLO	EOLVR	EVLRO
ROLEV	RLOVE	RVOEL	REVOL
ROLVE	RLOEV	RVOLE	REVLO
ROVEL	RLVEO	RVEOL	RELOV
ROVLE	RLVOE	RVELO	RELVO
ROELV	RLEOV	RVLOE	REOLV
ROEVL	RLEVO	RVLEO	REOVL

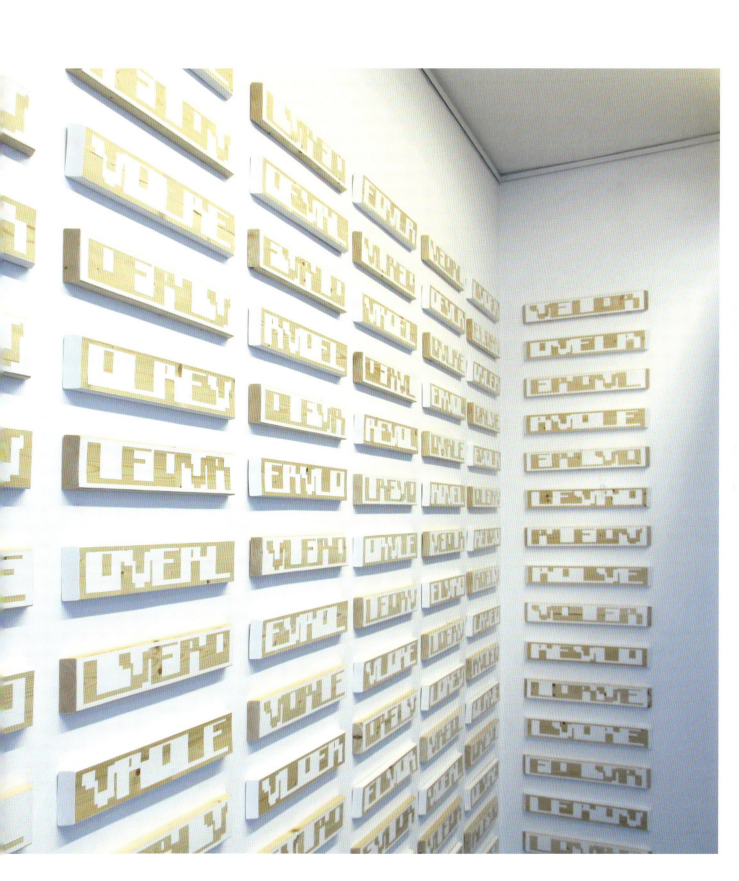

S. 48, *LOVER* (Permutations-Zeichnung), 2009
Graphit/Papier, 21 x 14,8 cm

S. 48/49, 51, *LOVER* (Detail), 2009

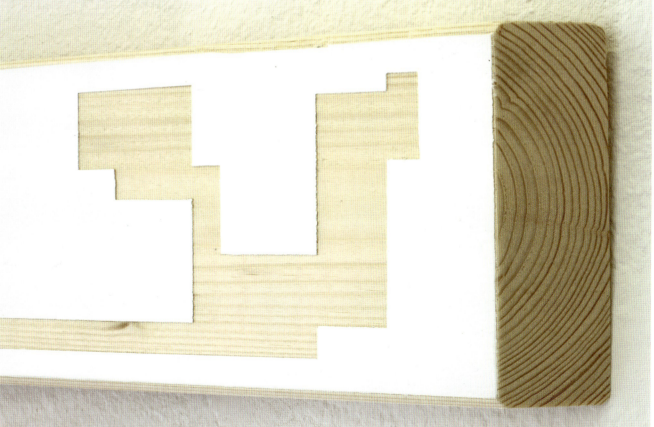

S. 52, 53, *LOVER* (Detail), 2012

S. 54/55, *LOVER* (Installationsansicht), 2012
Acryl/Vinyl/Seekiefer/Holz
je 9,5 x 57 x 2,5 cm, 120-teilig plus zwei Transportobjekte

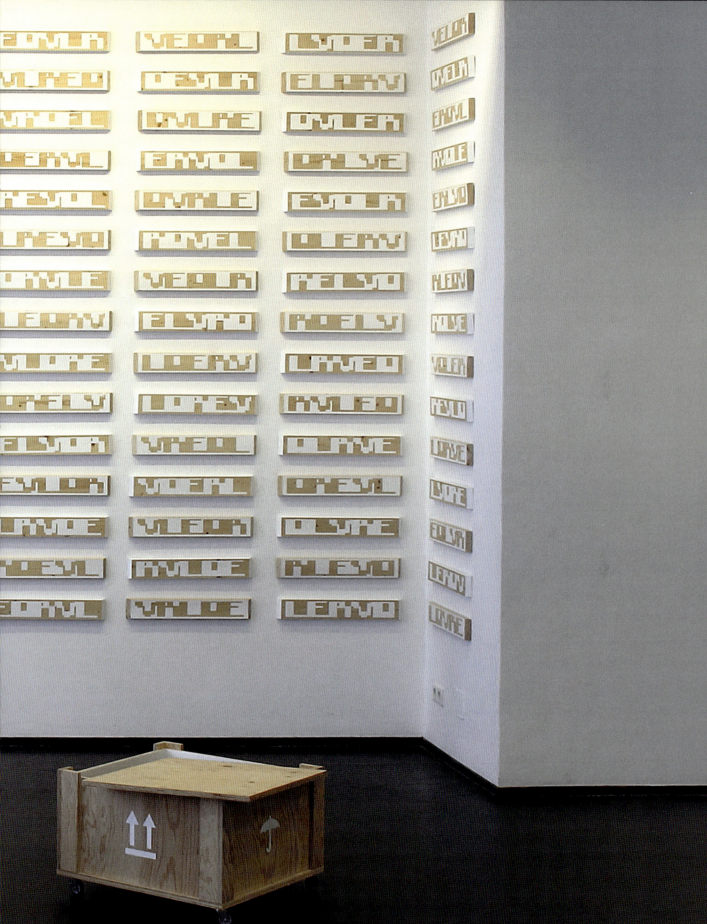

Lover, 2009
Acryl/Vinyl/Seekiefer
130 x 100 x 2 cm

LANDKARTEN ZWISCHEN WISSENSCHAFT UND KUNST

Jan Mokre

Karten sind von Menschen geschaffene, graphische Repräsentationen geographischer Phänomene, die es ermöglichen, räumlich definierte Strukturen darzustellen sowie Zusammenhänge und Wechselwirkungen sichtbar zu machen. Sie zeigen oft über die Topographie hinaus Aspekte unserer Welt, die in der Realität gar nicht sichtbar sind, zum Beispiel die Besitzverhältnisse an Grund und Boden oder, um ein ganz anders geartetes Beispiel heranzuziehen, geologische Strukturen.

Anspruchsvolle Kartographen bemühen sich, ein nachvollziehbares, aber auch ein die unterschiedlichen Elemente harmonisch zusammenfassendes Bild der Welt zu schaffen. Sie begreifen dabei ihre Arbeit als eine Verbindung zwischen exakter Wissenschaft und Kunst – wissenschaftlich in Bezug auf die Datengrundlage und künstlerisch in Bezug auf die Wiedergabe derselben mittels bestimmter Methoden und Gestaltungsmittel. Kartographen wählen nicht nur die wiederzugebenden Informationen aus, sondern sie bestimmen auch das Kartenformat, die Lage des dargestellten Gebietes in diesem und die zur Anwendung kommenden Formen und Symbole; sie entscheiden über die Stärke der Linien und die Farben der Flächen. Kartographen verfügen also über Gestaltungsfreiheit und über Gestaltungsmacht und diese einsetzend, schaffen sie mit ihren Karten keine exakten Abbilder der Welt sondern eigene Welten. Aber – dürfen sie das überhaupt?

Es ist nicht möglich, die Realität vollständig, übersichtlich und maßstabsgetreu auf ein Blatt Papier zu bannen und zudem noch mit erläuternden Symbolen und lesbaren Beschriftungen zu versehen. Daher wird bei jedem kartographischen Herstellungsprozess generalisiert. Generalisieren bedeutet, Entscheidungen darüber zu treffen, welche Informationen lagegenau auf der Karte aufscheinen, welche in ihrer Lage etwas verschoben dargestellt werden

MAPS BETWEEN SCIENCE AND ART

Jan Mokre

Maps are man-made artifacts, representations of geographic phenomena that make it possible to depict spatially defined structures as well as to reveal interrelationships and interplays. They often show more than just topography, disclosing aspects of our world that in reality are not visible at all, as for instance, property and ownership relations or to take a completely different example, geological structures.

Sophisticated cartographers go to great pains to create an image of the world that is clear and harmonious but also brings together the very different elements of the world. They consider their work as a combination of precise science and art – scientific with regard to the data on which it is founded and artistic in terms of the rendition of this data by means of specific methods and creative tools. Cartographers do not just select the information to be rendered, they also determine the format of the map, the location of the area depicted here and the forms and symbols that are used. They decide how thick the lines are and what colors the areas are rendered in. Cartographers thus have creative freedom and leeway and by using this they do not create exact copies of the world in their maps but separate worlds. But are they actually allowed to do this?

It is not possible to capture reality in its entirety, clearly and realistically, true to its dimensions, on a sheet of paper and to also add explanatory symbols and legible descriptions. In each production process of a map there is some generalization. To generalize means to make decisions on which information appears true to location on the map and which is depicted a bit off kilter, moved into the background or completely neglected. Generalizing also means to decide in which form and in which size information is to be renderend

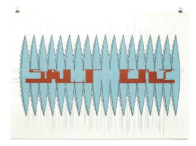

Bright Laborator, 2007
Siebdruck/Papier, 70 x 100 cm

und welche in den Hintergrund treten bzw. überhaupt vernachlässigt werden. Generalisieren bedeutet weiterhin zu entscheiden, in welcher Form und in welcher Größe Informationen auf der Karte wiedergegeben werden. Dafür gibt es verschiedene Möglichkeiten und handwerkliche Methoden – Bewerten, Typisieren, Klassifizieren, Kategorisieren, Zusammenfassen, Vergrößern, Verdrängen, Vereinfachen – über die ich hier nicht im Detail berichten möchte.

Nur ein Beispiel: Wenn sich in einem schmalen, von hohen Bergen eingeschlossenen Tal ein Fluss mit einer Schifffahrtslinie und eine Anlegestelle, eine mehrgleisige Eisenbahnverbindung, ein Bahnhof, eine mehrspurige Straße und darüber hinaus Wohngebäude und ein Gewerbegebiet befinden, muss der Kartograph, um alle diese Elemente auf einer kleinmaßstäbigen Karte sichtbar machen zu können, die Entscheidung treffen, das Tal in der kartographischen Darstellung zu verbreitern. Ist es aber sein Hauptanliegen, auf seiner Karte topographische Genauigkeit zu erzielen, wird er die verschiedenen thematischen Elemente zusammenfassen oder graphisch vereinfachen müssen. Genau so verhält es sich mit den auf Karten verwendeten Symbolen. Diese werden nicht maßstabsgetreu dargestellt, sondern sind fast immer überproportional größer als die Merkmale, die sie repräsentieren.

Generalisieren hat demnach zur Folge, dass – damit entscheidende Informationen nicht in einem Gewirr von Details untergehen – die Karte notwendigerweise ein ausgewähltes, unvollständiges Bild der Realität wiedergibt. Eine Karte, die keine Generalisierungen enthält, ist weitestgehend nutzlos – dennoch, jede Karte lügt, indem sie Dinge verschweigt. Die Generalisierung stellt, sozusagen, eine Notlüge dar.

Aber die Kartographen „lügen" auch aus anderen Beweggründen. Karten enthalten Geoinformationen von hohem wirtschaftlichen und militär-strategischen Wert, und veröffentlichte Karten verbreiten dieses Wissen. Dementsprechend lassen sich immer wieder staatlich administrative Bemühungen nachweisen, die Verbreitung ökonomisch bzw. militärisch relevanten Wissens zu verhindern. Am offenkundigsten geht dies durch strenge Geheimhaltung.

on a map. For this there are various possibilities and technical methods – assessing, typifying, classifying, categorizing, summarizing, enlarging, suppressing, simplifying – about which I will refrain from describing in detail here.

Just one expample. If, in a narrow valley enclosed by high mountains, there are a river that has a ferry boat line, a docking point, a multi-track train connection, a train station, a multi-lane road, and also residential buildings and a commercial area, the cartographer must decide to enlarge the valley in the cartographic rendition to be able to visualize all these elements on a small-scale map. But if the cartographer is mainly interested in obtaining topographical precision with his/her map, the various thematical elements will have to be summarized or graphically simplified. The same is true for the symbols used on the maps. These are almost always proportionately larger than the features they are supposed to represent than if these features were rendered in keeping with their real dimensions.

If the decisive information is not to disappear in a sea of details, generalizing must thus mean that the image of reality rendered by the map is by necessity a selected, incomplete one. A map that contains no generalization is largely useless – yet every map lies by concealing things. Generalizing is a sort of white lie.

But cartographers also "lie" for other reasons. Maps contain geo-information of high economic and military-strategic value and published maps disseminate this knowledge. Thus it can again and again be proven that governments try to stop knowledge that is economically and militarily relevant from being disseminated. This is most obviously done by strict confidentiality. Notes about the sea routes leading to America or India, discovered in the early modern age, were kept strictly secret for almost two centuries. In Portugal sharing maps that were guarded like treasures could even be punished by death.

Aufzeichnungen über die in der frühen Neuzeit entdeckten Seewege nach Amerika bzw. Indien blieben zum Beispiel fast zwei Jahrhunderte lang strengster Geheimhaltung unterworfen; in Portugal stand damals auf die Weitergabe der wie Schätze gehüteten Karten sogar die Todesstrafe.

Da es jedoch auf Dauer kaum möglich und auch nicht sinnvoll ist, alle Karten geheim zu halten, wurden und werden Karten auf unterschiedliche Weise manipuliert. Dazu werden relevante Karteninhalte gelöscht oder verfälscht, das heißt, entweder bewusst falsch eingezeichnet oder es werden zur Tarnung falsche Bezeichnungen in die Karte aufgenommen. So verschwinden zum Beispiel Militärflughäfen in unzugänglich gekennzeichneten Naturschutzgebieten und aus Atomkraftwerken werden unauffällige Industrieanlagen. Eine spezifische Form der Kartenverfälschung liegt in der absichtlichen Verzerrung des Gitternetzes, um die Abnahme richtiger geographischer Koordinaten von der Karte zu verunmöglichen. Die Verfälschung von Karten aus Gründen militärischer Sicherheitserwägungen hat eine sehr lange Tradition und wird allgemein als durchaus legitim angesehen, so wie auch die „Versorgung" des militärischen Gegners mit gefälschtem Kartenmaterial, um ihn zu verwirren oder zu falschen Schritten zu verleiten, als eine spezielle Art der Desinformation und somit als Erfolg nachrichtendienstlicher Tätigkeit gilt. Auch zur Abwendung befürchteter, terroristischer Angriffe auf Regierungsgebäude, militärische Einrichtungen sowie strategisch wichtige Orte werden Karten verfälscht.

Der Vollständigkeit halber sei erwähnt, dass die Problematik der seit der frühen Neuzeit zu beobachtenden Geheimhaltung und Kartenmanipulation natürlich längst auch im Bereich der digitalen Geodaten und deren Bereitstellung auf öffentlich zugänglichen Satellitenbildern und digitalen Geodatenträgern, wie zum Beispiel Google-Earth, durch Verfremdungen und sogenannte Verpixelungen Einzug gehalten hat.

Karten können aber auch Propagandainstrumente der Mächte in Politik und Wirtschaft sein. Staaten, Lobbygruppen, multinationale Konzerne und internationale Organisationen bedienen sich dieses Mediums, um den

However, since it was hardly possible and also did not really make sense to keep all maps secret, maps have been manipulated in a variety of ways. Relevant map contents have been omitted or distorted, that is, either deliberately drawn falsely or wrong names have been included in the map to hide something else. For instance, military airports disappear in nature reserves marked as unaccessible and nuclear power plants are transformed into inconspicuous industrial facilites. One particular form of map distortion pertains to the grid network to make it possible to deduce correct geographical coordinates from the map. The falsification and distortion of maps motivated by military considerations regarding security has a very long tradition and is generally considered as legitimate since the military opponent is provided with distorted map material to cause confusion or to induce wrong steps, this being a special form of disinformation that can also be seen as a successful measure related to intelligence corps activity. Maps are also distorted to ward off feared terrorist attacks against government buildings, military facilities as well as strategically significant locations.

For the sake of completeness, I would like to point out that the issue of confidentiality and manipulation of maps that can be observed since the beginning of the modern age has meanwhile entered the world of digital geo-data and the media where they are presented in publicly accessible satellite images and digital geo-data media such as Google Earth where data can be manipulated and pixelled.

Maps can also be used as propaganda instruments of powers in politics and business world. Countries, lobby groups, multinational corporations and international organizations employ this medium to convey their world view, to extend or consolidate their power. Cartographers have a number of methods at their disposal – one being the selection of the projection of a map. The spheric surface of the earth cannot be projected onto a flat surface, that is a sheet of paper, without distorting angles and/or areas.

Kartennutzern ihre Weltsicht zu vermitteln, um Macht aufzubauen bzw. zu festigen. Den Kartographen stehen dazu zahlreiche Methoden zur Verfügung, eine liegt bereits in der Wahl der Kartenprojektion. Die Projektion der sphärischen Erdoberfläche in die Ebene, also auf ein Blatt Papier, lässt sich nicht ohne Verzerrungen von Winkeln und/oder Flächen bewerkstelligen. Seriöse Kartographen wählen immer die Projektion, die die geringsten Missverständnisse bei der Karteninterpretation hervorruft – durch bewusste Wahl einer bestimmten, eigentlich unpassenden Projektion lassen sich demgegenüber aber auch ganz gezielt Fehlinterpretationen in Bezug auf die Vergleichbarkeit von Flächen oder Entfernungen bewirken.

So wurden die Karten in den westlichen Propagandaschriften in der Zeit des Kalten Krieges oft in der sogenannten Mercator-Projektion gezeichnet. Diese gibt die nördlichen Flächen der Erde stark vergrößert wieder – so wirkte die Sowjetunion, mathematisch exakt gezeichnet, gegenüber Westeuropa übermächtig und besonders bedrohlich. Oder ein anderes Beispiel für die Instrumentalisierung von Karten als Propagandamittel: Immer wieder lässt sich beobachten, dass strittige Grenzen oder Gebiete auf Karten als gegeben, also unstrittig, dargestellt werden – oft jedoch in unterschiedlichen Varianten, je nachdem, wo und von wem die Karte hergestellt wurde.

Das bedeutet also, dass auch sogenannte amtliche Karten ideologisch geprägte Darstellungen der geographischen Realität sind, die weder als wertfrei noch als objektiv und auch nicht als wissenschaftlich gelten können. Regierungen und die von ihnen abhängigen Verwaltungen praktizieren Einflussnahme, Zensur und Kontrolle in Bezug auf Karten aber nicht nur nach außen sondern auch nach innen zur Durchsetzung bzw. Bekräftigung gesellschaftlicher oder politischer Ziele. Und die Kartographen setzen dies um – zum Beispiel durch Weglassung oder durch beschönigende Darstellung bestimmter unbequemer Informationen bzw. Verbindungen und Beziehungen.

Kartographen „lügen" aber auch aus Eigennutz: Um die unrechtmäßige Verbreitung ihrer Werke zu verhindern, legen sie sogenannte „Copyright Traps" an. So werden

Serious cartographers always select the projection that causes the least misunderstandings in map interpretation – by deliberately selecting a certain, really unsuitable projection misinterpretations can by contrast be created with regard to the comparability of areas and distances.

Maps in western propaganda writings in the Cold War period were often drawn in the so-called Mercator projection. This renders the northern areas of the earth in very enlarged form – the Soviet Union thus appeared, drawn mathematically exact, to be overpowering and particularly threatening towards the West. Or to take another example for the instrumentalizaton of maps as a means of propaganda: again and again one can observe that undisputed boundaries or regions on maps are depicted as given, that is undisputed – often however in various forms depending on where and by whom the map was produced.

This means that even so-called official maps are ideologically influenced representations of geographic reality, which can neither be seen as value-free or objective or as scientific. Governments and the administrations dependent on them exert influence, censorship and control with regard to maps but not just to the outside but also to the inside to enforce or back their social or political goals. And the cartographers implement this – for instance by omissions or by embellishing representation of unpleasant information or connections and relations.

Cartographers, however, also lie for their own interests: to prevent the illegal diffusion of their works they lay so-called "copyright traps". For instance, fictive streets are entered in maps so that if push comes to shove the illegal cooptation of cartographic work by competitors can be proven. Apart from this, there is still another well-known form of map falsification: A British military cartographer who was commissioned with mapping a small island in the Aegean in 1903, deliberately selected fictive names for mountain peaks in the assumption that his obviously unpopular boss captain

zum Beispiel in Stadtpläne fiktive Straßen eingezeichnet, um im Fall des Falles das unrechtmäßige Übernehmen kartographischer Basisarbeit durch kopierende Konkurrenten nachweisen zu können.

Darüber hinaus gibt es noch eine weitere, bekannte Form der Kartenverfälschung: Ein britischer Militärkartograph, der 1903 mit der Kartierung einer kleinen Insel in der Ägäis beauftragt worden war, wählte in der richtigen Annahme, dass dies seinem offenbar ungeliebten Vorgesetzten, Kapitän Corry, nicht auffallen würde, absichtlich fiktive Bezeichnungen für Berggipfel, die zusammengesetzt und rückwärts gelesen, den Satz ergeben: „may Corry be damned" und verewigte auf diese Weise seine Antipathie auf einer gedruckten, amtlichen britischen Admiralitätskarte.

Der Kartograph Richard Ciacci aus Boulder zeichnete in die Karte des US-Bundesstaates Colorado einen fiktiven Berg namens „Mount Richard" ein, um sich damit ein persönliches Andenken zu verschaffen. Es dauerte zwei Jahre bis die Verfälschung entdeckt wurde. Oder – in der 2007 publizierten 103. Auflage des unter dem traditionsreichen Namen „Putzger" bekannten Historischen Atlasses findet sich auf der Karte „Mitteleuropa im Zeitalter der Reformation" südwestlich von Bleiburg in Kärnten der Ort „Hobbingen". Diesen Ort gab es dort nie, sehr wohl aber in J. R. R. Tolkiens Fantasy-Trilogie „Der Herr der Ringe". So wie auch das, im erwähnten Atlas an der Donau in Ungarn eingezeichnete „Bruchtal", als „Versammlungsort der späteren Ringgemeinschaft", Tolkiens Fantasie entstammt. Diese Verfälschungen entsprechen einer langen Tradition humorvoller Kartographen. Die fiktiven Orte wurden für folgende Auflagen aus den Druckvorlagen gelöscht, die Schuldigen ermittelt und hoffentlich nicht allzu hart bestraft.

Kartographische Darstellungen sind durch verschiedene Einflüsse und Filter bestimmte menschliche Produkte, die stark von der Weltsicht des Kartographen bzw. der seiner Auftraggeber bestimmt sind. Das bedeutet, die Karte ist ein Spiegel der Gesellschaft, der politischen, sozialen, technischen und ökonomischen Situation ihrer Entstehungszeit; sie beinhaltet auch eine ideologische und/oder politische Dimension.

Corry would not notice this. These names that could be read together and backwards produced the sentence: "may Corry be damned", thus eternalizing in this way his antipathy on a printed official admiralty map.

Cartographer Richard Ciacci from Boulder, Colorado drew a fictive mountain named "Mount Richard" into the map of US state Colorado to create a personal memorial for himself. It took two years for this manipulation to be discovered. Or in the 103rd edition of the venerable German historical atlas known as "Puzger", there is a map titled "Central Europe in the Age of the Reformation" where one finds a town called "Hobbingen" located southwest of Bleiburg in Carinthia. This town, however, never existed there but could actually be found in J.R.R. Tolkien's fantasy trilogy "The Lord of the Rings". Furthermore "Bruchtal" on the Danube in Hungary, also to be found in the mentioned atlas as a "place where the later ring community convened" likewise is a product of Tolkien's imagination. These falsifications are in keeping with a long tradition of humorous cartographers. The fictive places were deleted from printer's copies for subsequent editions, the culprits were tracked down and punished, though hopefully not too severely.

Cartographic representations are human artifacts that are informed by various influences and filters which in turn are strongly informed by the world view of the cartographer or of his/her clients. This means that a map is a reflection of society, of the political, social, technical and economic situation of time in which it evolved. It also contains an ideological and/or political dimension.

Cartographic representations are, however, also depictions of subjective production. By virtue of the selection of data, forms and colors, the cartographer lends his/her depiction of reality an individual face; his/her creative freedom moves between art and manipulation. Cartographers can accentuate several lines as opposed to others – a thick red arrow simply does not convey the same message as a thin blue one – irrespective of

Dark Star, 2007
Siebdruck/Papier, 70 x 100 cm

Kartographische Darstellungen sind aber auch Abbilder subjektiven Schaffens. Durch die Wahl der Daten, Formen und Farben, verleiht der Kartograph seinem Abbild der Realität ein individuelles Gesicht; seine Gestaltungsfreiheit bewegt sich dabei zwischen Kunst und Manipulation. Kartographen können einige Striche gegenüber anderen verstärken; ein dicker roter Pfeil vermittelt nun einmal nicht dieselbe Botschaft wie ein dünner blauer – unabhängig davon, wie beide in der Kartenlegende verbal erklärt sind. Und die Kartographen können Flächen durch die ihnen zugewiesenen Farben bestimmte Wertigkeiten verleihen und auf diese Weise zum Beispiel politische Aussagen treffen. Ganz abgesehen davon, dass den sprachlichen Elementen einer Karte, Toponymen und anderen Benennungen und Beschreibungen, immense Bedeutung für die Kartenrezeption zukommt. Wie ein Künstler, der in einem Werk die Realität abbilden möchte, wertet der Kartograph nicht nur zahlreiche Quellen aus, sondern er verlässt sich auch auf seine umfassenden Kenntnisse und Erfahrungen. Der Kartograph „weiß", wie seine Karte aussehen soll und gestaltet diese entsprechend.

Ein letzter Aspekt: Karten enthalten natürlich auch Fehler, die ihre Ursache in fehlerhaften Datengrundlagen, in Unwissenheit bzw. Unachtsamkeit des Kartenzeichners, aber auch in versehentlichen Verfälschungen im Produktionsprozess haben können. Fehler von Kartographen können zum Beispiel darin bestehen, dass auf einer Karte ein wichtiger Ort nicht eingezeichnet wird; Mängel im Produktionsprozess können dazu führen, dass durch schlecht abgestimmte Grautonrasterung in der Vorlage unterschiedlich gestaltete Flächen auf der gedruckten Karte nicht voneinander unterschieden werden können.

Obwohl die Kartenherstellung also von zahlreichen Einflüssen, bis hin zur Manipulation geprägt ist, die Karten nur scheinbar die Wirklichkeit der Welt abbilden, wird ihnen jedoch in der Regel von den Kartennutzern unwillkürlich Objektivität zugebilligt. Sie bieten aber auch nur Interpretationen der Wirklichkeit. Und daher erlaube ich mir, in Abwandlung eines berühmten Zitates, die abschließende Empfehlung: Vertrauen Sie keiner Karte, die Sie nicht selbst manipuliert haben.

how both are verbally explained in the map legend. And cartographers can also lend areas certain qualities by assigning them certain colors and thus, for instance, make political statements. And this completely apart from the fact that the linguistic elements of a map, toponyms and other designations and descriptions have immense meaning for the reception of a map. Like an artist who would like to depict reality in a work, the cartographer does not just evaluate a number of sources, he/she also draws on his/her vast knowledge and experience. The cartographer "knows" how his/her map should look and designs it accordingly.

One final aspect: Maps do of course also contain mistakes that may be due to their being based on faulty data, on the ignorance or negligence of the cartographer but also in accidental distortions in the production process. A cartographer's mistake might, for instance, be failing to indicate an important location on a map. Shortcomings in the production process could result in it now being possible to distinguish differently designed areas on the printed map because of a poorly coordinated halftoning of gray shades.

Even if the production of maps is subject to a number of influences all the way to manipulation, and maps only seemingly depict the reality of the world, map users as a rule automatically attribute objectivity to them. Yet maps also offer only interpretations of reality. And thus many I end by paraphrasing a famous quote: Do not trust any map that you didn't forge yourself.

Deep Blue, Faltobjekt, 2007
Siebdruck/Papier, Ø 29 cm

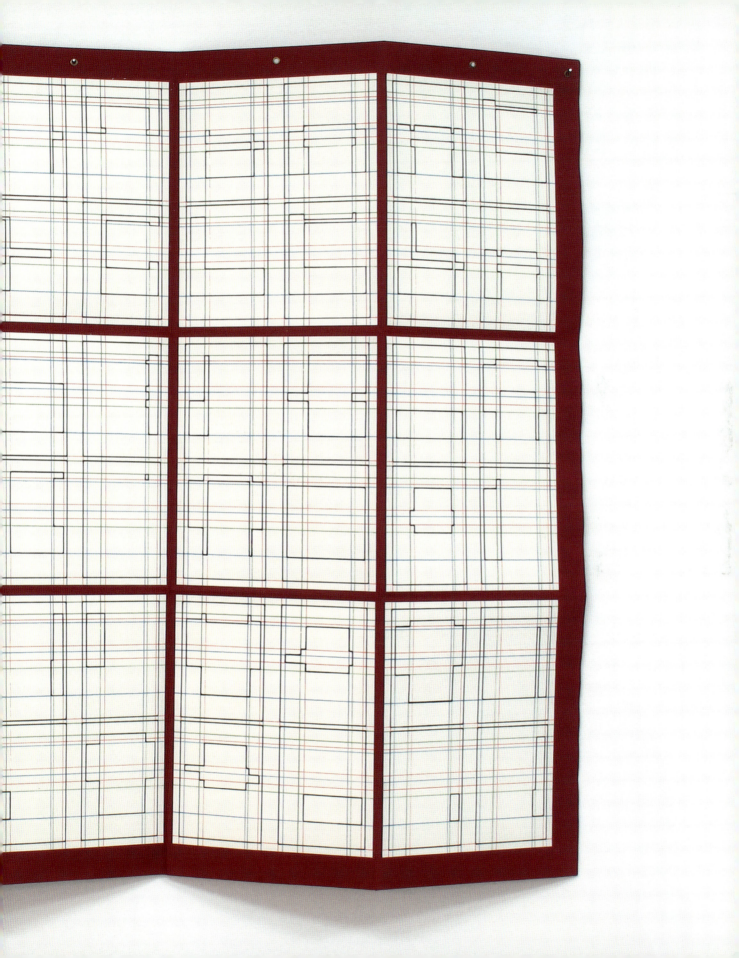

S. 66/67, 69, *Adapted Land*, 79 x 121 cm, 2007
Siebdruck/Papier/Leinen

ERIC KRESSNIG 2012

S. 70/71/72, *Langes Stück*, 2012
Messing-Objekt, 2,6 x 2,6 x 52 cm

S. 73 Zeichnung, S. 74 (Detail)
S. 75, Objektansicht, Acryl/Vinyl/Holz/Aluminium
Display, 100 x 59,5 x 59,5 cm

Untitled, 2012, Holzschnitt, je 50 x 60 cm

GEFLECHT.

Thomas Ballhausen

You wrote a book about yourself
The people left it on the shelf
You'll write another one
Now, you've got a story that's worth talking about

Belle and Sebastian: Put the Book Back on the Shelf

Ich gehe davon aus, dass auch die folgenden Begebenheiten als Fallgeschichte zu behandeln sein werden. Ich möchte darüber hinaus davon ausgehen, dass ein weiteres Verbrechen begangen werden soll. Die versiegelten Anweisungen, die ich schon vor langer Zeit, ganz zu Beginn meiner Karriere als Chefkartograph des Kombinats, entgegengenommen habe, sprechen sehr deutlich davon. Entsprechend habe ich mich vorbereitet und den größeren Teil meines Lebens darauf ausgerichtet. Meine Arbeit am Kolleg habe ich immer mit Sorgfalt und Umsicht durchgeführt, ich habe alle üblichen Fehler vermieden, habe keine Spuren hinterlassen und bis man mich überführt, habe ich das perfekte Verbrechen begangen. Die Vermessung des Reichs, an der ich ungeachtet der jüngsten Ereignisse festhalte, betreibe ich als ein Projekt der Ausdehnung von Wahrheit oder zumindest als eine Unternehmung, die sich einer Sache verschrieben hat, die wir gemeinhin für Wahrheit halten. Im Erstellen von Karten liegt eine Zuweisung von Bedeutungen begründet. Das Schreiben der Karte, denn ich schreibe sie ebenso wie ich sie zeichne, ist für mich ein Ermittlungsprozess und zugleich eine verbindliche Vorgabe, wie das Leben zu bewältigen ist. Im jeweiligen Dokument vermischen sich die Möglichkeiten, die Karte ist ein einziges Geflecht, das in jeden Zustand gebracht werden kann. Wenn ich Skizzen anfertige, eine Tätigkeit, die ich immer noch gerne ausführe, lege ich Punkte fest, trage Daten ein. Das konstruierte Raster werfe ich aus wie ein Fischer sein Netz. Es gilt Geduld zu beweisen und

NETWORK.

Thomas Ballhausen

You wrote a book about yourself
The people left it on the shelf
You'll write another one
Now, you've got a story that's worth talking about

Belle and Sebastian: Put the Book Back on the Shelf

I assume that the circumstances to be described in the following should be treated as a case study. I would also like to assume that a further crime is to committed. The sealed instructions that I received at the very beginning of my career as the lead cartographer of the combine are certainly testimony of this. And so I prepared myself accordingly and devoted a larger part of my life to this. I have always done my work at the college with the greatest of care and circumspection. I have avoided all the normal mistakes, I have not left any traces and by the time I am convicted I will have committed the perfect crime. The surveying of the empire, which I am sticking to in spite of the most recent events, is something I pursue as a project of disseminating the truth or at least as an undertaking that has committed itself to a cause that we generally take to be the truth. The writing of the map, for I am writing it just as much as I am drawing it, is for me a process of investigation and at the same time provides a binding standard of how to master life. In this document the options are mixed, the map is one single network which can be transferred to every state. When I create sketches, an activity that I still like to engage in, I define dots. I enter data. I cast the constructed grid like a fisher does his net. Patience must be shown and one has to wait and see how the space gets caught in this grid. In my work I was constantly moving back and forth between the

zuzusehen, wie sich der Raum darin verfängt. In meiner Tätigkeit bin ich zwischen den entferntesten Orten des Kombinats und meinem Arbeitszimmer in der Hauptstadt, hier bei den Sammlungen im Kartenhaus, ständig hin und her gependelt. Wenn ich einen Blick auf meine Unterlagen werfe, die sich im Verlauf der Jahre angesammelt haben, muss ich mir eingestehen, dass sie Belege für einen vorsätzlichen und glücklichen Missbrauch meiner Mittel sind, vermesse ich die Gebiete doch nicht nur, trage ich ja auch zu ihrer Zähmung und Überwachung bei. Es erfüllt mich in meinen schwachen Momenten mit ein wenig Stolz, dass meine Aufzeichnungen ohne die Hässlichkeit der Bewohner der von mir erfassten Ländereien auskommen. Ich verberge sie in der Eleganz einer Legende, in der Genauigkeit und Verwechselbarkeit meiner Schrift. Das Schreiben meiner Karte verlangt nach schwerem Gerät, nach Ausrüstung und – zumindest in meinem Fall und Aufgabengebiet – auch nach einer Anzahl von Büchern, die mich in einem eigenen Koffer, der zu einem kleinen Arbeitsregal aufgeklappt werden kann, überallhin begleiten. Es ist notwendig, die wesentlichsten Dinge jederzeit nachschlagen zu können. Natürlich gibt es die gesetzlichen Vorgaben über die Titel, die noch in den kleinsten Garnisonsstädten vorhanden sein müssen. Neben statistischen Jahrbüchern, religiösen und juristischen Schriften – wobei der Unterschied zwischen diesen mitunter schwer auszumachen ist – finden sich eine geraume Anzahl weiterer Bände in den verbindlichen Angaben. Da ist etwa Mirandas vierbändiges Werk *Die Reisen besonnener Knaben*, wobei aber stets einzelne Bände dieser Ausgabe zu fehlen scheinen. In der Liste der Bücher finden sich auch Spechts *Kunst des Lügens und Schau-Spielens*, Mitchells *Bildtheorie*, Peakes *Kleine Schule für soldatisches Zeichnen* oder Osbornes *Das Element des Verbrechens*. Ich war immer überrascht, dass sogar Mordaunts *Wetterkunde*, das einzige Werk dieses ins Exil abgedrängten Tunichtguts, immer noch darauf zu finden ist. Von ihm, dem als Bestrafung ein Teil seines Verstandes geraubt und in eine ihm unerreichbare Flasche gesteckt wurde, blieb nur dieses Buch, was aus ihm wurde, ist

most remote places of the combine and my study in the capital, here next to the collections in the map house. When I cast a glance at my material that has accumulated over the years, I must admit that they are evidence for a deliberate and fortunate abuse of my means. I not only survey the regions, I also contribute to controlling and watching over them. In my weak moments it endows me with a bit of pride that my notes were able to make do with the ugly inhabitants of the estates I documented. I conceal them in the elegance of a legend, in the precision and unmistakability of my writing. Writing my map calls for a heavy device, for equipment – and at least in my case and my field of tasks – also for a number of books that accompany me everywhere in a small suitcase that when opened can serve as a small working shelf. It is important to be able to look up the most important things at any moment. Of course, there are the legal stipulations on titles that have to be present even in the tiniest garrison towns. Apart from statistical yearbooks, religious and legal texts – the difference between the two sometimes being difficult to ascertain – there is a great amount of further mandatory reading cited, as for instance, Miranda's four-volume work *Journeys of Considerate Boys* with individual volumes of this edition always appearing to be missing. In the list of books one also finds Specht's *Art of Lying and Acting*, Mitchell's *Pictorial Theory*, Peake's *A Short Introduction to Military Drawing* and Osborne's *The Element of Crime*. I was always surprised to see that even Mourdant's *Meterology*, the only work by this rapscallion who was forced into exile, can still be found in the list. Only this book remained of him – he who as punishment was robbed of part of his mind which was placed in a bottle out of his reach. To this day no one knows what became of him. By contrast it seems easier to understand why Bell and Miller's reworking of Doolittle's classic *Fable of the Small Stars* is so popular in the combine and readily available.

bis heute unklar. Einleuchtender scheint mir hingegen, warum Bell und Millers Überarbeitung von Doolittles Klassiker *Fibel der kleinen Sterne* überall im Kombinat beliebt und erhältlich ist. Die für mich aber wichtigsten Veröffentlichungen könnten aber wohl unterschiedlicher nicht sein. Da ist einerseits meine Arbeitsgrundlage, die dreibändige Ausgabe von Liddells *Atlas der bekannten und unbekannten Welt*, den ich in zwei Exemplaren besitze. Im Verlauf meiner Arbeit ist eines davon zum Nachschlagen gänzlich unbrauchbar geworden, ist es doch über und über mit Korrekturen, Anmerkungen und eingeklebten Skizzen übersät. Einzig eine Seite ist noch unbeschrieben, die Seite, in der die Zitadelle der uns beherrschenden Schwestern verzeichnet stehen sollte. Nur die Legende weist diese Leere aus, die ich in meiner Neuedition des Atlanten zu füllen habe. Ich war nicht unglücklich, diese letzte, noch nicht bewerkstelligte Aufgabe durch zahlreiche Recherchen und andere Arbeiten bislang hinauszögern zu können. Der immer noch andauernde Krieg mit den Eisenmännern machte eine Vielzahl zumindest mir willkommener Verbesserungen notwendig, mussten doch vermehrt anstelle von ausgedehnten Siedlungen nun Ruinen, Trümmerfelder und städtische Reste sorgfältig erfasst werden. Für diese erwähnte, abschließende Herausforderung war mir nun andererseits auch ein Werk von nicht zu unterschätzender Hilfe, das meine Kollegen bislang schändlich vernachlässigt hatten – die autobiografischen Aufzeichnungen Spontinis. Eher zufällig war ich schon vor Jahrzehnten auf diesen nur fragmentarisch erhaltenen Bericht gestoßen, der von den Herausgebern des Texts wohl aus purer Hilflosigkeit *Aphorismen* betitelt worden war. Spontinis Buch hat mir alles gesagt und beigebracht, was ich über meine eigene Beschaffenheit, meinen Mangel an Natürlichkeit und Willen wissen musste.

Die schon erwähnten, erwirkten Aufschübe und ständig verschobenen Abgabetermine haben mich im Rahmen meiner Bearbeitung von Liddells Buch immer wieder zu dieser leeren Seite zurückgeführt, vor der ich

The publications I find most important could, however, hardly be any more different. There is, for one, my working copy, the three-volume edition of Liddell's *Atlas of the Known and the Unknown World* which I own in two copies. While working, one of them became completely unserviceable as a reference book, it being completely covered with corrections, notes and pasted in drawings. Only one page remains free, the page on which the citadel of the sisters ruling over us should be listed. Only the legend identifies this void which I will have to fill in my new edition of the atlas. I was not unhappy about being able to delay this still neglected task with all the research and all the other work that was left to do. The war that is still waging with the Iron Men made it necessary to make a number of corrections that at least I welcomed, since now it was not extensive settlements but rather ruins, fields of debris and remains of towns that had to be carefully documented. For this challenge that came last there was now a work that proved to be of inestimable help to me, one that my colleagues have to date shamefully neglected – the autobiographical notes by Spontini. It is more by chance that already decades ago I had hit upon this account that has remained largely fragmentary, which the editors titled *Aphorisms* – probably out of a sense of total helplessness. Spontini's book told and taught me everything what I need to know about my own disposition, my lacking instinctiveness and will.

The delays I already mentioned, the constantly extended submission deadlines again and again led me back to this empty page in connection with my reworking of Liddell's book which I no longer wish to shy away from. Actually the atlas is close to perfect, in the sense that it is accessible and veils the facts of today. Yet fleshing out this specific page is the only point where I can actually chime in, the only moment where I can contribute something

nun nicht länger zurückschrecken will. Eigentlich ist der Atlas, so wie er zugänglich ist und die Tatsachen unserer Gegenwart verschleiert, nahezu perfekt. Doch das Ausfüllen dieser bestimmten Seite ist der einzige Punkt, an dem ich wirklich einhaken, der einzige Moment, an dem ich etwas von Bedeutung beitragen kann. Ich habe mich, die Anweisungen immer wieder und immer wieder neu studierend, gefragt, ob das tatsächlich so gewünscht, von den Schwestern so gewollt sein kann. Diese eine neue Karte zu verfertigen, wird den Lauf der Welt verändern, eben weil sie zeigen wird, wie sich die Zeit im Raum niederschlägt. Schließlich soll sich hier ein realer Raum abgebildet finden, der für alle gut sichtbar sein wird. Die Karte gestaltet den Raum und der Ort wird sich ihr unterwerfen, die physische Beschaffenheit wird sich, so bin ich mir sicher, unter meinen Strichen verändern, seine ursprüngliche Form verlieren und eine neue gewinnen. Ich werde beginnen, die Dinge zu bestimmen, die Möglichkeiten der Orientierung vorzugeben. Ich werde die Karte in der Bewältigung dieser Aufgabe zum Territorium machen und beweisen, dass zumindest hier das Kombinat noch intakt ist. Mit der Vermessung dieser bislang ausgesparten Leerstelle, mit dieser Nachzeichnung der Lücke, werde ich Liddells Werk vervollständigen und damit aber auch das Geheimnis der Zitadelle aufheben. Wenn ich meinen Auftrag erfülle, bringe ich meine Herrinnen zu einem eigentlich unverdienten Ende. Sie hätten sich, so ist es meine feste Überzeugung, schon einen glorreicheren Untergang verdient als durch mich. Zumindest das, wenn schon sonst nicht sehr viel über sie bekannt ist, steht für mich fest. In den Geschichten und Verlautbarungen heißt es, dass es immer drei Schwestern waren, die die Geschicke des Kombinats lenkten. Bei der Verschwörung und dem darauffolgenden Mordkomplott, das nun auch schon wieder mehrere Jahre zurückliegt und sich nicht zufällig mit Mordaunts erzwungenem Exil verbindet, fiel eine von ihnen einem Attentat zum Opfer. Dem Volksglauben und den alten Schriften nach war nur sie sterblich. Die beiden anderen Schwestern verließen danach nie wieder die Zitadelle hier in der Hauptstadt, in der sie

significant. Again and again studying the instructions anew, I have wondered whether this was actually the way it was supposed to be, if the sisters wanted it to be this way. Completing this new map will change the course of the world, as it will show how time is reflected in space. Finally a real space should be depicted here, which is easily visible for all. The map designs space and the place will yield to it, the physical appearance will change under my lines, this I am sure of, will lose its original shape and assume a new one. I will begin to define things, to set down the possible orientations. I will turn the map into a territory while tackling this task and show that at least here the combine remains intact. By surveying this vacant space that has not been taken into account until now, I will complete Liddell's work and thus also reveal a secret of the citadel. When I fulfill my mission I will bring my mistresses to an end that is not really deserved. It is my real conviction that they would have deserved a more dignified demise that through me. At least, if not much is known about them, that much is certain for me. In the stories and statements it is claimed that there were always three sisters who had been responsible for the destiny of the combine. In the conspiracy and the subsequent murder plot, which is now also several years old and is not just coincidentally linked to Mordaunt's forced exile, one of them succumbed to an assassination attack. According to popular belief and the old writings only she was mortal. Afterwards the two other sisters never left the citadel again here in the capital, in which they sit like snakes in the midst of their well-ordered world map, if not within their well-ordered wold. Again and again one would hear that following the murder their power was broken and that in the wake of this they would carry hand-held spindles with them all the time and visible to all so as to commemorate their loss. This public display of emblems of mourning and fallibility which I couldn't quite explain would have been absolutely

wie Schlangen inmitten ihrer wohlgeordneten Weltkarte, wenn schon nicht inmitten ihrer wohlgeordneten Welt, sitzen. Man hörte immer wieder davon, dass nach dem Todesfall ihre Macht gebrochen war und sie zur Erinnerung an ihren Verlust danach, jederzeit und für alle sichtbar, Handspindeln bei sich trugen. Dieses mir nicht gänzlich nachvollziehbare, öffentlich zur Schau getragene Zeichen der Trauer und Fehlbarkeit wäre in den frühen Tagen, den Hochzeiten ihrer Herrschaft schlicht undenkbar gewesen. Ihr Einfluss war deutlich im Schwinden und nahm immer weiter ab, auch wenn selbst heutzutage nur hinter vorgehaltener Hand darüber gesprochen wird. Kaum jemand wird in die Zitadelle, hier im Herzen der Hauptstadt und ihres Einflussbereichs, vorgelassen, kaum jemand hat sie von innen gesehen. Deutlicher kann man die im Norden jüngst errichtete Mauer, die jetzt schon nach ihrem Architekten den Namen *Aurelianische Mauer* trägt, sehen. Sie ist mir ein Eingeständnis der Unsicherheit, ein Beleg, dass auch die Hauptstadt nun nicht mehr außerhalb der sich ausdehnenden Gefahrenzone liegt, dass auch sie Teil des Kriegsgebiets werden könnte. Die Angst scheint ihren Weg zu jedem Zuhause zu finden, und ich muss gestehen, ich habe die Mauer nicht gerne vermessen und gezeichnet, sie nur widerstrebend in die Karten eingetragen.

Ich habe ein zutiefst geometrisches Verständnis der Dinge, vom Konzept der Wirklichkeit und der Abstraktion der Beziehungen, aller Beziehungen. Über diesen Umstand bin ich nicht unglücklich, wobei ich es in manchen Momenten schon bedauert habe, dass jeder meiner Mitmenschen einen guten Grund zu haben scheint, um sich von mir abzuwenden. Selbst von meinen engsten Vertrauten erwarte ich es mir nicht anders, mache ich mir doch Bilder, die der Meinung der Allgemeinheit nach nicht zulässig wären, schlicht nicht zulässig sind. Diese Bilder sind immer bei mir, selbst wenn ich erschöpft neben einer anderen Person einschlafe und doch noch bemerke, wie die von mir auf dieser Person angebrachten Zeichnungen und Male schwächer werden und

unthinkable in the early days, the weddings of their rule. Their influence was clearly waning and continued to do so, even if even today people only talk about it in hushed voices. Hardly anyone is allowed to enter the citadel, here in the very heart of the capital and its realm of influence, hardly anyone has seen it from within. More visible is the wall that was recently erected to the north, which now already bears the name of its architect *Aurelian Wall.* For me it is a confession of insecurity, evidence that even the capital now no longer lies outside the expanding danger zone which could also become part of the war area. Fear seems to find its way into every home, and I must admit that I didn't enjoy measuring and drawing the wall, and it was only reluctantly that I entered it in the maps.

I have a profoundly geometric understanding of things, of the concept of reality and the abstraction of relationships, of all relationships. I am not unhappy about this state of affairs, even though there have been moments in which I have regretted that each of my fellow human beings seems to have a good reason to turn away from me. I don't expect it to be any different with the closest of my associates, as I do make myself images that in public opinion would simply not be admissible. This imagery is always with me, even when I fall asleep exhausted next to another person and am yet able to notice how the drawings and marks that I attach to this person become ever weaker and finally disappear, and this person becomes for me in my delusion and my conviction someone who I once knew, but all further meaning is lost. I proceed in a calculating way, touch as if by accidental the finger on my left hand where there should actually be a ring. So I proceed calculatingly and question what is real. Authenticity strikes me as so questionable at times, as the fake and artitical is hidden in everything real. Where is the lock that is supposed to

schließlich verschwinden, diese eine Person für mich in meinem Wahn und meiner Überzeugung zu jemandem wird, den ich einmal gekannt habe, jede weitere Bedeutung aber geht verloren. Ich gehe berechnend vor, berühre wie zufällig den Finger meiner linken Hand, an dem eigentlich ein Ring sitzen sollte. Ich gehe also berechnend vor und befrage, was echt ist. Authentizität scheint mir mitunter so fragwürdig, ist doch das Falsche und Gekünstelte in all dem Wirklichen versteckt. Wo ist der Verschluss, den es zu öffnen gilt, ich möchte ihn inzwischen, mit dem Verschwinden meiner Geduld und der Veränderung meiner Strategien, gewaltsam aufreißen. Meine Gefühle haben sich in letzter Zeit geändert, ich habe ganz vergessen, was ich alles daran hasse und ich kann es kaum noch erwarten, meinen Weg zur Zitadelle anzutreten. Aus dem Rückzug wird auch in dieser Situation etwas entstehen, vielleicht auch nur ein souveränes Scheitern, aus dem ich einen erbärmlichen, kleinen Sieg ableiten kann. Das Leben wird sich in dieser Arbeit, die nun kurz vor ihrer schrecklichen Vollendung steht, nicht nur spiegeln, es wird sich darin gestaltet finden. Sobald ich die gewaltigen Festungsanlagen passiert habe, werde ich die innere Zitadelle im Bewusstsein betreten, meinen Auftrag zu erfüllen oder meinem Nachfolger, der mir noch unbekannt ist, zum Opfer zu fallen wie mir mein in die Tage gekommener Vorgänger. Hier wird die Geschichte enden.

be opened? Meanwhile, now that my patience has disappeared, along with any change in my strategies, I would like to tear it open with force. Recently my feelings have changed. I have completely forgotten everything that I despise about it and can hardly wait to begin my march to the citadel. In this situation the retreat will give way to something, perhaps only to a sovereign failure from which I can derive a small, pathetic victory. In this work which is just awaiting its horrible completion, life is not just reflected, it also finds shape here. As soon as I have walked past the imposing fortress, I will enter the inner citadel with a sense of having fulfilled my mission or having succumbed to my successor who is still unknown to me, as my aged predecessor succumbed to me a long time ago. Here the story will end.

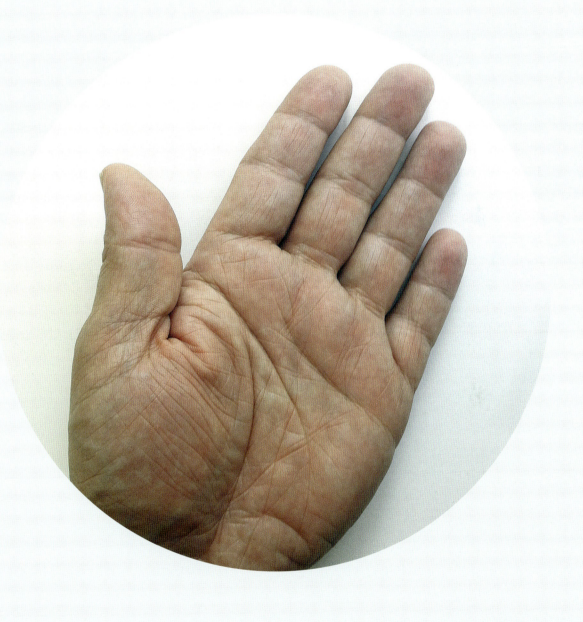

The door is an open field, 2003
Holz/Siebdruck/Plexiglas/Aluminium
200 x 66 x 64 cm (geschlossener Zustand)

S. 90/91, Entwurf

S. 92/93, Details

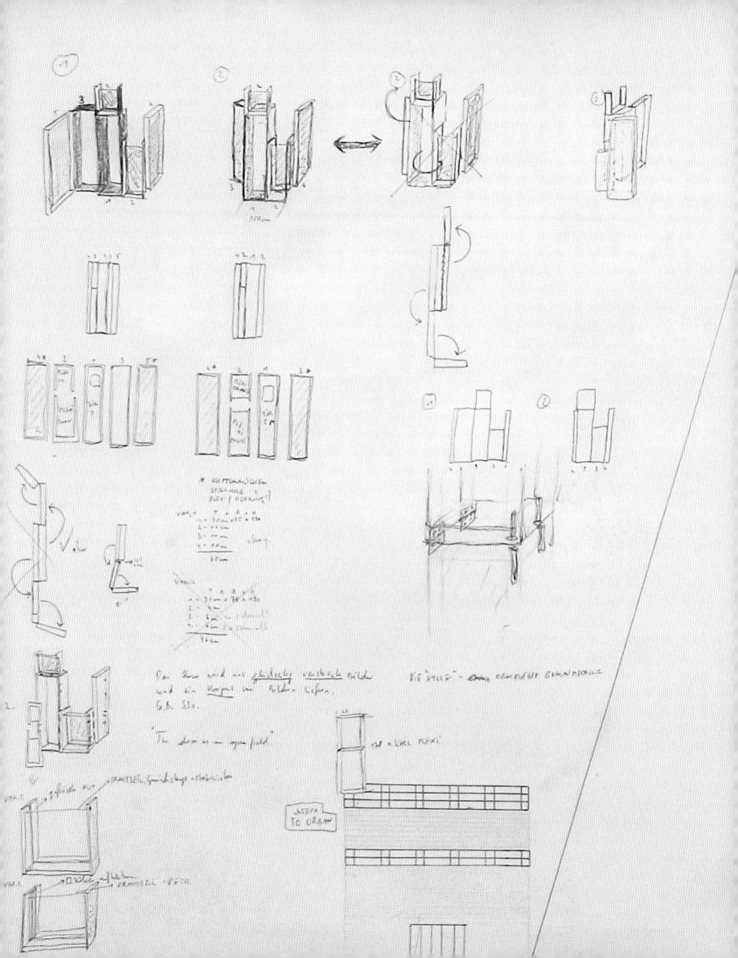

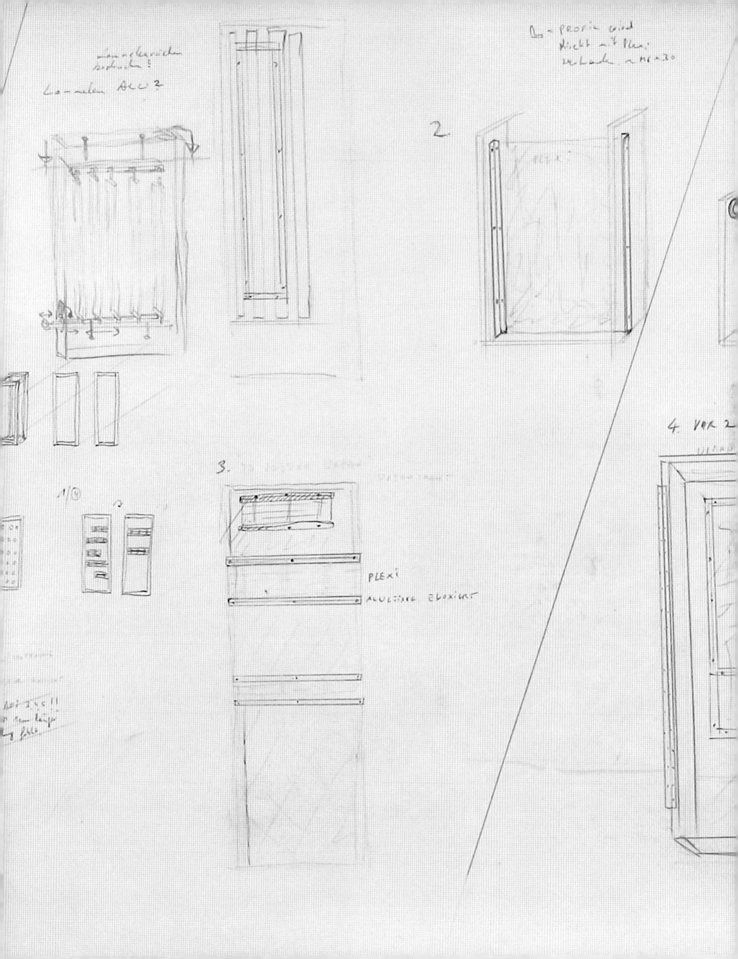

The door is an open field, 2003
Holz/Siebdruck/Plexiglas/Aluminium
(offener Zustand)

S. 96/97, Werkdemonstration

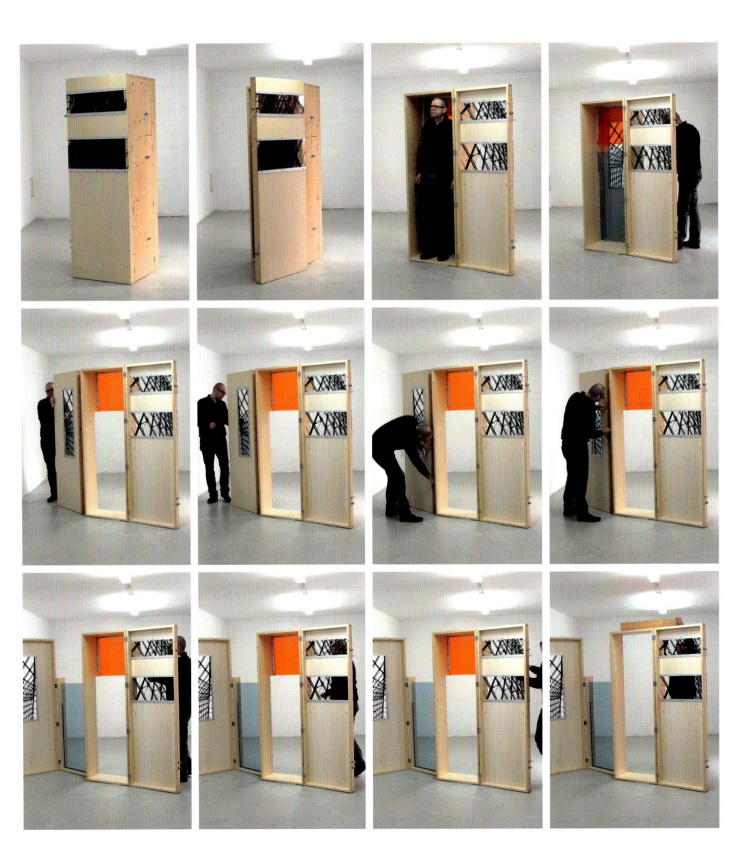

DIRTY MINIMAL
MALEREI ZWISCHEN KONZEPT UND INTUITION

Martin Engler

> *„Die Hauptsache, die mit der Malerei nicht stimmt, ist, dass sie eine rechteckige Fläche ist, die man flach vor der Wand platziert."*
>
> Donald Judd: Specific Objects

Diese auf wunderbare Weise schroffen und wenig – wenn nicht gar keinen – Widerspruch duldenden Thesen Donald Judds sind bald ein halbes Jahrhundert alt und gelten gemeinhin als eine der wesentlichen Grundlegungen der amerikanischen Minimal Art – und eines Großteils der nachfolgenden Malerei diesseits wie jenseits des Atlantiks. Über alle Verwerfungen der letzten Jahrzehnte hinweg beschreiben sie bis heute die Eckpfeiler jenes Ausstiegs aus dem Bild, an dem sich die Malerei in der Nachfolge Barnett Newmans, Mark Rothkos oder Ad Reinhardts mit unterschiedlichsten Vorzeichen und Herangehensweisen, vor allem aber mit immer neuen Lösungen abarbeitet. Judds Absage an das Tafelbild und seine Feier der industriellen Materialität in der 3. Dimension eröffnen auch den Malereien, Objekten, skulpturalen Setzungen Eric Kressnigs einen spannenden Resonanzraum. Mehr noch, erst über dieses „Tertium comparationis" erwächst seinem komplexen, im positiven Sinne verwirrend vielschichtigen Werk eine sinnstiftende Struktur.

Um was es geht, ist nach wie vor der Raum – als zentrale malerische Unwägbarkeit. Jener Moment, in dem die gemalte Fläche sich öffnet oder verschließt, das Bild Objekt wird oder die Fläche affimiert. Immer wieder von neuem wird jener spezifische Ort der Malerei vermessen, der sich einer letztgültigen Beschreibung entzieht. Die Arbeiten Eric Kressings umspielen mit Stringenz und Insistenz, im großen, wie im kleinen Format, als Tafelbild oder als komposites, raumgreifendes Objekt eine der

DIRTY MINIMAL
PAINTING BETWEEN CONCEPT AND INTUITION

Martin Engler

> *"The main thing wrong with painting is that it is a rectangular plane placed flat against the wall."*
>
> Donald Judd: Specific Objects

These claims made by Donald Judd that are wonderfully acerbic and tolerate little if any contradiction will soon be half a century old. They are generally seen as one of the main underpinnings of Minimal Art – and of a large number of the paintings to follow it on this and the other side of the Atlantic. Over and beyond all the fault lines of the past decades, they continue to describe the core of the break with the easel painting which was something that was to preoccupy painters after Barnett Newman, Mark Rothko and Ad Reinhardt. New solutions were again and again presented under the most varied circumstances and using different approaches. Judd's renunciation of the easel painting and his celebration of industrial materiality in the third dimension also opened up a fascinating resonating cavity for Eric Kressnig's paintings, objects, sculptural configurations. And what is more, it was only with this "Tertium comparationis" that his complex oeuvre, which is confusingly multifarious in a positive sense, was able to create a meaningful structure.

The major issue is still spatiality – as the central painterly imponderable. Each moment in which the painted surface opens up or closes, the picture becomes an object or the surface is affirmed. Again and again the specific place of painting is measured anew – a locus that evades any definitive description. With great stringency and persistence, Eric Kressing's pieces – both large and small formats, easel paintings or composite, room-filling objects – revolve around one of the most fascinating

Dome, 2009
Acryl/Vinyl/Seekiefer
4 Elemente je 63 x 60 x 60 cm

spannendsten Fragen der Malerei der Moderne bis in unsere Gegenwart: Wie lässt sich die Malerei, das Bild in seinem nie enden wollenden Zwiespalt zwischen Raum und Fläche, zwischen Fiktion und Objekt, beschreiben, wenn die Bilder ihrer klassischen Räumlichkeit im Sinne eines Abbilds der Realität verlustig gingen?

Der vierteiligen, 2,52 Meter hohen Holz-Skulptur *Dome*, 2009, und *Untitled*, 2010, deren sechs Leinwandquadrate ein monumentales Wandbild formulieren, unterliegt die identische räumliche Ambivalenz. Bildträger und Bild, reale und malerische Struktur kommen nicht zur Deckung. Zwischen Malerei und Objekthaftigkeit, zwischen Illusionsraum und real in der Tiefe des Gehäuses gestaffelten Farbflächen, wird eine produktive Spannung deutlich. Diese Arbeiten sind Objekt und Malerei in einem, kehren ihre 3. Dimension selbstbewusst nach außen und sind zugleich mit jeder Faser ihrer malerischen und objekthaften Präsenz der Tradition des Tafelbilds verpflichtet. Sie sind materialsichtig und zugleich in subtiler Weise malerisch, sind abstrakt und real im selben Atemzug. Faszinierende Verwirrspiele, die Räume öffnen und zugleich verschließen, den Betrachter ins Bild locken, nur um diesen (Bild)Raum umgehend hermetisch in die Fläche zu bannen. Komposite Bildarchitekturen, die sich gegenseitig neutralisieren.

Für und mit Donald Judd waren die Dinge zumindest vorläufig klar entschieden. Nur wenig Malerei befand der Minimalist, als Erfinder der „Spezifischen Objekte", die den Illusions-Raum konsequent hinter sich lassen wollten, überhaupt erwähnenswert. Der – gleichwohl in der modernistischen Maler-Wolle gewirkte – Bilderstürmer wollte der Kunst den Raum konsequent austreiben, allerdings nur, um im nächsten Schritt die zweidimensionale Flächigkeit endgültig zu verlassen. Er rief das Zeitalter des „Real Space" und der „Dreidimensionalen Objekte" aus, die weder Fisch noch Fleisch sein wollten, weder Skulptur noch Malerei – und doch von beiden Gattungen das Beste in sich vereinten. Dieser neue – echte, reale – Raum, den diese Objekte postulieren, entpuppt sich allerdings

questions of modern painting even today: How can painting, the picture within its never-ending dichotomy between space and surface, between fiction and object, describe something, if the paintings have lost their classical spatiality in the sense of a depiction of reality?

The four-part 2.52 meter high wooden sculpture *Dome*, 2009, and *Untitled*, 2010, whose six canvas squares constitute a monumental wall piece, is based on this identical spatial ambivalence. Picture support and picture, real and painterly structure, do not converge. Between painting and object hood, between illusionary space and surfaces of color that are really staggered into the depth of the housing, a productive tension becomes visible. These pieces are object and painting in one, revealing their 3rd dimension self-assuredly to the outside and are at the same time with each fiber of their painterly and object-like painting supports and painting, real and painterly structure do not converge. Between painting and object hood, illusionary space and color surfaces that are really staggered into the depth of the housing, a productive tension clearly emerges. These pieces that are object and painting in one self-assuredly display their third dimension to the outside and are also indebted with each fiber of their painterly and object-like presence to the tradition of the easel painting. They are clearly material and at the same time painterly in a subtle way, abstract and real in the same breath. Fascinating, confusing charades that both open up and close spaces, luring the viewer into the painting only to immediately capture this (pictorial) space hermetically ion the surface. Composite pictorial architectures that neutralize each other.

For and with Donald Judd things had been clearly decided on at least for the time being. The minimalist, as inventor of the "Specific Objects" that wanted to radically break with the illusionary space, saw only little material as worth mentioning. The iconoclast – albeit one who was cut of the same modernist painter's cloth – sought to consistently rid art of space only to take leave of the two-dimensionality, the planarity in the next step. He ushered

Untitled (Detail), 2010
Acryl/Leinen
360 x 540 x 16 cm

als nicht weniger illusionistisch und sinnlich, als höchst vielfältig zwischen Wahrnehmung und Realität oszillierend, denn der Raum der Malerei.

An dieser Stelle, spätestens, kommen die Bildobjekte Eric Kressnigs ins Spiel. Der Gegensatz von Malerei und dem „Specific object" Judds hat sich im Laufe der Jahrzehnte verflüchtigt. Was wir vorfinden, ist eine hybride Malerei, die den Paradigmenwechsel der Minimal Art auf das Bild zurück wendet. Eine Malerei, wenn man so will, der Ambivalenz. Eine Ambivalenz allerdings, die das Unentschiedene, Offene als Chance begreift, der das Sowohl-als-Auch stilbildend wird. Eine raumgreifende Arbeit wie *The door as an open field*, 2003, macht diesen Moment des Hybriden greifbar als offene, wandelbare Setzung, als realiter sich öffnende und verschließende Form. Schon die Tür-Metapher verdeutlicht, dass die Bereiche durchlässig werden sollen, die Grenzen sich verflüssigen. Der malerisch-skulpturale Bastard aus Holz, Aluminium, Siebdruck und Plexiglas ist nicht nur Fläche und Objekt, Malerei und Skulptur in einem, sondern zugleich in der Lage seinen ästhetischen Aggregatzustand spielerisch zu wechseln. Eine monumentale „Boite en valise", die das künstlerische Potenzial von Kressnigs Œuvre in einer mobilen Setzung kondensiert. Vor allem zeigt sich, dass dies keine stringente, teleologische Entwicklung ist. Die Dinge ereignen sich parallel. Dieses Werk entwickelt sich gleichzeitig und mit unterschiedlichen Geschwindigkeiten in divergierende Richtungen, ohne Gefahr zu laufen, sich selbst zu verlieren.

Was aus diesen vielfältigen und weit reichenden Rochaden zwischen der Kunst und ihrem Raum resultiert, ist aber vor allem ein selbstbewusst auftretender Betrachter, der in ganz neuer Form zwischen dem Bild und seinen vielfältigen räumlichen und materialen Möglichkeiten vermittelt. Wenn wir also nach der Spezifik der Arbeiten Eric Kressnigs fragen, kann der Betrachter, der auf neue Weise mit den Bildern und ihrem Raum in Beziehung tritt, nicht außen vor bleiben. Im Gegenteil, der aktive suchende Blick des Betrachters wird zur zentralen Instanz,

in the age of "real space" and the "three-dimensional objects" that sought to be neither fish nor fowl, neither sculpture nor painting – and yet incorporated, united the best of both genres. This new – genuine, real – space that these objects postulated, however, proved to be no less illusionist and sensual, oscillating in a highly diverse way between perception and reality, as the space of painting

Here at the latest Eric Kressnig's pictorial object come into play. The contrast between painting and Judd's „speciifc object" has evaporated over the decades. What we now find is hybrid painting, which turns the paradigm shift of Minimal Art back to the picture. A painting of ambivalence, as one could describe it. However, it is an ambivalence that sees the indecisive, the open as an opportunity, which is constitutive of style in both directions. A room-filling piece such as *The door as an open field*, 2003, made this aspect of hybridity tangible as an open transformable placement, as a form that actually opens and closes. Already the door metaphor illustrates that the areas should become permeable, the boundaries dissolving. The painterly-sculptural hybrid made of wood, aluminum, silk-screen and plexiglass is not just a surface and an object, painting and sculpture in one, but also capable of playfully changing its aesthetic aggregate state. A monumental „boite en valise" that condenses the artistic potential of Kressnig's oeuvre in a mobile installation. Above all it becomes clear that this is not a stringent, teleological development. Things happen in parallel. This work develops simultaneously and with various speeds in different directions, without succumbing to the danger of losing itself.

What results from this variegated, far-reaching castling between art and its space, is first and foremost a viewer who is able to mediate in a new self-assured way between the painting and its diverse spatial and material possibilities. In trying to define the specific quality of Eric Kressnig's works, then the viewer who is relating in a new way with the paintings and the space surrounding them does not remain on the outside. On the contrary, the

wenn wir uns auf die Spur dieses malerischen Raums begeben, der den Bildern und Objekten Eric Kressnigs einen neuen, hybriden Aggregatzustand verleiht.

Ursprung der Malerei sind im Falle der Bilder Eric Kressnigs ebenso logische – wie bis zur Banalität – einfache Systeme: Bild und Objekt werden vordergründig zur malerischen Rechenoperation, zum Planspiel mit Farbe und Struktur, das auf mathematische, geometrische oder auch lexikalische Koordinatensystem verweist. Mit wissenschaftlicher Unbestechlichkeit wird jeder Arbeit ein System aus Farbe und Form zu Grunde gelegt, aus dem ein Bildraum entsteht, der 2. und 3. Dimension miteinander verschränkt.

In der Lektüre dieses Systems der seriellen Bildgenese erklären sich die Bilder im Zwiegespräch, ohne sich jemals wirklich zu entschlüsseln. Sie scheinen Frank Stellas – wunderbar schlichter – Definition seiner minimalistischen Streifenbilder eine Wendung in die Malerei unserer Gegenwart zu geben: „A diagram is not a painting. [...] I can make a painting from a diagram, but can you?" Ein offenes System, das keine letztgültigen Antworten kennt. Das auch im farbmächtigsten Bild immer noch sichtbare Koordinatensystem verweist bis zuletzt auf den wesentlichen Status dieser Bilder, als arbiträre, nur vorläufig gültige, liquide, jedoch gleichsam momentan zur Ruhe kommender Lösungen des Systems.

Die Schriftarbeiten Kressnigs verdeutlichen diesen Punkt mit Nachdruck. In *Lover*, 2009, werden die fünf Buchstaben des Wortes einer rabulistischen Kombinatorik unterworfen. Eine endlose Flut vorderhand unverständlicher Zeichen in einer Ordnung behauptenden Struktur, die ihr strukturalistisches Angebot aber bewusst nicht einlöst. Die Systematik lässt sich vielleicht irgendwann erahnen. Bedeutung, sinnstiftender Nachvollzug, allerdings, stellt sich nicht ein. Das System kippt in seiner Abundanz ins Unübersichtliche, was nicht gleichbedeutend ist mit dem Chaotischen. Das Zeichen entblößt sich seiner Lesbarkeit und im Überangebot der Sinneinheiten, geht der Sinn verloren. Der „Liebhaber" verliert sich so im Rapport der Malerei, die Sinnlichkeit und Erotik des Wortes wird überdeckt von der geometrischen Abstraktion aus Farbe und Form.

beholder's actively searching gaze becomes a central authority, when we embark upon the trace of this painterly space which lends Eric Kressnig's paintings and objects a new, hybrid aggregate state.

The origins of painting are, in the case of Eric Kressnig's painting – are systems that are both logical and also simple to the point of banality: Picture and object clearly become an act of painterly calculation, a planned game with color and structure referring to mathematical, geometric or even lexical system of coordinates: reflecting the unerring scientific precision, each work is based on a system of color and form, out of which a pictorial space emerges in which the second and third dimensions merge.

In the interpretation of this system of a serial development of the picture, the paintings explain each other in a dialogue without ever really deciphering themselves. They seem to give Frank Stella's – wonderfully simple – definition of his minimalist stripe paintings a twist to contemporary painting: "A diagram is not a painting. [...] I can make a painting from a diagram, but can you?" An open system which knows no definitive answers. The coordinate system which is still visible in the most imposing color paintings refers to the essential status of these paintings, as an arbitrary, only temporarily valid, fluid yet momentarily resting solutions provide by the system.

Kressnig's text pieces illustrate this aspect emphatically. In *Lover*, 2009, the five letters of the word are subject to quibbling combinatorics. An endless deluge of incomprehensible signs in a structure asserting order but one that does not deliberately deliver on its structuralist offerings. The systematics can perhaps be surmised at some point. Meaning, references allowing for such meaning to be reconstructed, however, do not appear. In its abundance the system tilts, tumbles into confusion, which is not synonymous with chaos. The sign reveals itself in its legibility and in the plethora of sensual units, sense is lost. The "lover" thus loses himself in the rapport of paining, the sensuality and eroticism of the word is obscured by the geometric abstraction of color and form.

Ein Verlust allerdings, der nur ein vorläufiger ist. Denn hier kommt der neue, neu ins Spiel eintretende Betrachter zu Zuge. Nur er kann sich der kollabierenden Systematik entgegenstemmen, in dem er lokalen Sinn erzeugt. So wird im Werk Eric Kressnigs nicht nur Donald Judd, sondern auch Frank Stella neu gelesen. Er tritt zwar nicht an die Stelle des Künstlers, aber er kann einen passageren Diskurs etablieren. Die rabulistische Dynamik des automatisierten Buchstaben-Verdrehens, wird momentan geerdet. Sinn entsteht im Dialog. Malereien, Skulpturen, Objekte und Installationen Kressnigs werden so zur selbstreflexiven Zeitmaschine, die Verlorengeglaubtes und Korrumpiertes wieder möglich machen und mit neuem Sinn erfüllen.

Der theoretische Diskurs der 2. Avantgarde, der Minimal und Conceptual Art, wird in seiner Strenge gebrochen. Neben Geometrie und industriell aufgetragener Farbe, neben Materialechtheit und Objekthaftigkeit kommt das Spielerische und Zufällige wieder zu seinem Recht. Dafür, für eine bewusste Abweichung vom gestrengen Formalismus, steht nicht zuletzt die spezifische, im ersten Angang irritierende Farbigkeit Kressnigs: Nicht industrielle, ungemischte, eindeutige Farben kommen zum Zug sondern eine faszinierend reichhaltige Palette. Unmerklich abgemischtes Weiß, gebrochene Tonalitäten, Mischfarben, die der reinen Leere bewusst widersprechen.

Die verwirrend sich entziehenden, ebenso strukturalen, wie spielerischen Wandarbeiten Sol LeWitts, um einen letzten der hier neu beleuchteten Minimal Künstler zu berufen, kommen in den Sinn. Die Arbeiten Kressnigs formulieren eine Re-Lektüre, eine Aktualisierung des Paradigmenwechsels der 1960er. Deren „Matter of factness" wird sinnlich gebrochen, die Systeme werden ausgehöhlt, die scheinbare Eineindeutigkeit geöffnet, für einen ästhetischen Mehrwert des Subjektiven, Unreinen, Suggestiven.

> *„Die Art von Kunst, die mich beschäftigt, möchte ich als konzeptuelle Kunst bezeichnen.[...] Diese Art von Kunst ist nicht theoretisch und keine Illustration von Theorien. Sie ist intuitiv."*
>
> Sol LeWitt: Pragraphs on Conceptual Art

A loss, however, that is only a preliminary one, since here the new observer, the new one coming into play, comes to the fore. Now s/he can counter the collapse of the system in which s/he creates local meaning. In Eric Kressnig's oeuvre, not just Donald Judd but also Frank Stella is interpreted in a new light. He does not take the artist's place but he is able to establish a temporary discourse. The quibbling dynamic of automatically twisting letters is grounded for a moment. Meaning emerges in dialogue. Kressnig's paintings, objects, and installations thus become a self-reflective time machine that make whatever was believed to be lost and corrupted possible again and imbued with new meaning.

The theoretical discourse of the 2nd avant-garde, of minimal and conceptual art, is undermined in its stringency. Apart from geometry and industrially applied paint, in addition to material authenticity and objectness, playfulness and the element of chance are reinstated. Kressnig's specific chromaticity, which at first glance is irritating, stands for this, for a deliberate break with a stringent formalism. Not industrial, unmixed, clearly recognizable colors are used but rather a fascinatingly rich palette. Unnoticeably mixed white, broken tonalities, mixed colors that deliberately contradict the pure emptiness.

The confusing, evasive, both structural and playful wall pieces by Sol LeWitt – to cite one last minimal artist to be reexamined in a new light – come to mind here. Kressnig's works formulate a re-interpretation, an updated version of the paradigm shift of the 1960s. The "matter-of-factness" is broken in a sensual way, systems are subverted, the seeming absolute clarity opened to allow an aesthetic added value of subjectivity, impurity and suggestiveness.

> *"I would like to call the type of art that interests me conceptual art [...] This type of art is not theoretical and it is not an illustration of theories. It is intuitive."*
>
> Sol LeWitt: Pragraphs on Conceptual Art

S. 104/105, *Ostend* (Aufbauansicht), 2010

S. 107, *Ostend* (Zeichnung), 2010

S. 108/109, *Ostend* (Permutations-Zeichnung), 2010
Graphit/Papier, je 21 x 14,8 cm

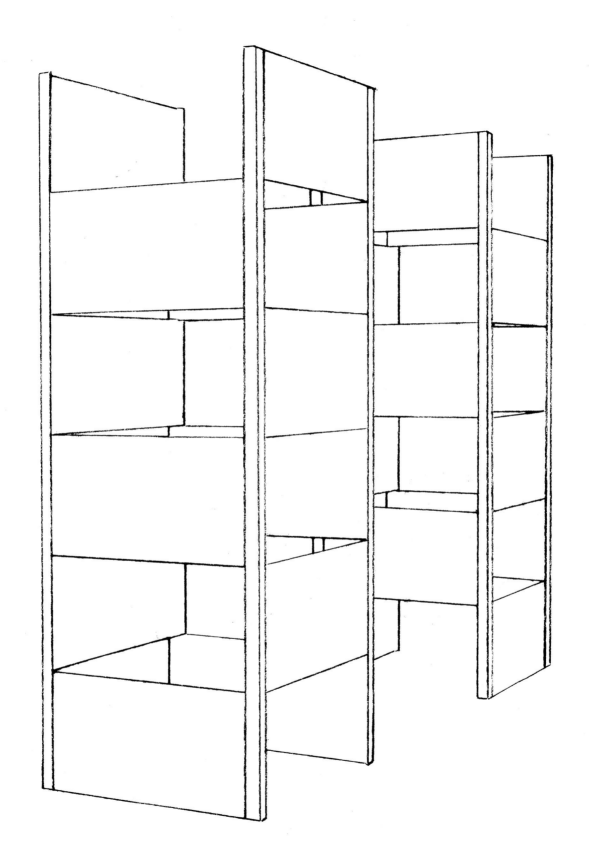

OSTEND OSETND OSNTED OSDTEN
OSTEDN OSETDN OSNTDE OSDTNE
OSTNED OSENTD OSNETD OSDETN
OSTNDE OSENDT OSNEDT OSDENT
OSTDEN OSEDNT OSNDET OSDNTE
OSTDNE OSEDTN OSNDTE OSDNET

OTESND OTSDNE OTNEDS OTDNSE
OTESDN OTSDEN OTNESD OTDNES
OTEDNS OTSEND OTNSDE OTDESN
OTEDSN OTSEDN OTNSED OTDENS
OTENSD OTSDNE OTNDES OTDNSE
OTENDS OTSDEN OTNDSE OTDNES

OETSDN OESTDN OENSTD OEDSTN
OETNDS OESNDT OENSDT OEDSNT
OETNSD OESNTD OENDTS OEDNTS
OETDSN OESDNT OENDST OEDNST
OETDNS OESDTN OENTDS OEDTSN
OETSND OESTND OENTSD OEDTNS

ONTSED ONSTDE ONDSTE ONETSD
ONTSDE ONSTED ONDSET ONETDS
ONTDSE ONSETD ONDEST ONEDTS
ONTDES ONSEDT ONDETS ONEDST
ONTESD ONSTED ONDTSE ONESDT
ONTEDS ONSTDE ONDTES ONESTD

ODTENS ODSENT ODESNT ODNSTE
ODTESN ODSETN ODESTN ODNSET
ODTNSE ODSTNE ODETNS ODNEST
ODTNES ODSTEN ODETSN ODNETS
ODTSNE ODSNET ODENTS ODNTSE
ODTSEN ODSNTE ODENST ODNTES

STENDO STNEDO STDNEO STODNE
STENOD STNEOD STDNOE STODEN
STEOND STNODE STDONE STONDE
STEODN STNOED STDOEN STONED
STEDON STNDEO STDEON STOEND
STEDNO STNDOE STDENO STOEDN

SETNOD SENODT SEONDT SEDNOT
SETNDO SENOTD SEONTD SEDNTO
SETDON SENTOD SEOTND SEDTNO
SETDNO SENTDO SEOTDN SEDTON
SETODN SENDOT SEODNT SEDONT
SETOND SENDTO SEODTN SEDOTN

SDONTE SDNOTE SDTNOE SDETNO
SDONET SDNOET SDTNEO SDETON
SDOETN SDNEOT SDTENO SDENTO
SDOENT SDNETO SDTEON SDENOT
SDOTNE SDNTOE SDTOEN SDEONT
SDOTEN SDNTEO SDTONE SDEOTN

SNOTDE SNTODE SNDTOE SNEDTO
SNOTED SNTOED SNDTEO SNEDOT
SNOEDT SNTEDO SNDETO SNEODT
SNOETD SNTEOD SNDEOT SNEOTD
SNODET SNTDEO SNDOET SNETOD
SNODTE SNTDOE SNDOTE SNETDO

SONTED SOTNED SOETND SODETN
SONTDE SOTNDE SOETDN SODENT
SONDET SOTDEN SOEDTN SODNET
SONDTE SOTDNE SOEDNT SODNTE
SONETD SOTEDN SOENTD SODTNE
SONEDT SOTEND SOENDT SODTEN

ENDOST ENODST ENSODT ENTSOD
ENDOTS ENODTS ENSOTD ENTSDO
ENDTSO ENOSDT ENSTOD ENTDOS
ENDTOS ENOSTD ENSTDO ENTDSO
ENDSOT ENOTSD ENSDOT ENTOSD
ENDSTO ENOTDS ENSDTO ENTODS

ETDNSO ETNDSO ETONDS ETSOND
ETDNOS ETNDOS ETONSD ETSODN
ETDONS ETNODS ETOSND ETSDNO
ETDOSN ETNOSD ETOSDN ETSDON
ETDSON ETNSDO ETODNS ETSNOD
ETDSNO ETNSOD ETODSN ETSNDO

EDSTNO EDTSNO EDNTSO EDONTS
EDSTON EDTSON EDNTOS EDONST
EDSOTN EDTOSN EDNOTS EDOSNT
EDSONT EDTONS EDNOST EDOSTN
EDSNOT EDTNSO EDNSOT EDOTSN
EDSNTO EDTNOS EDNSTO EDOTNS

ESTDNO ESDTNO ESNTDO ESOTND
ESTDON ESDTON ESNTOD ESOTDN
ESTODN ESDNTO ESNDTO ESODTN
ESTOND ESDNOT ESNDOT ESODNT
ESTNDO ESDOTN ESNODT ESONTD
ESTNOD ESDONT ESNOTD ESONDT

EONSTD EOSNTD EOTSND EODTSN
EONSDT EOSNDT EOTSDN EODTNS
EONTSD EOSTND EOTDSN EODNTS
EONTDS EOSTDN EOTDNS EODNST
EONDTS EOSDTN EOTNDS EODSTN
EONDST EOSDNT EOTNSD EODSNT

NOSTED NOTSED NOETSD NODETS
NOSTDE NOTSDE NOETDS NODEST
NOSDET NOTESD NOESTD NODSET
NOSDTE NOTEDS NOESDT NODSTE
NOSEDT NOTDES NOEDTS NODTSE
NOSETD NOTDSE NOEDST NODTES

NESTOD NETSOD NEOTSD NEDOTS
NESTDO NETSDO NEOTDS NEDOST
NESDOT NETDOS NEODTS NEDTSO
NESDTO NETDSO NEODST NEDTOS
NESODT NETODS NEOSDT NEDSOT
NESOTD NETOSD NEOSTD NEDSTO

NSEODT NSOEDT NSDOET NSTDOE
NSEOTD NSOETD NSDOTE NSTDEO
NSETDO NSODET NSDTOE NSTEOD
NSETOD NSODTE NSDTEO NSTEDO
NSEDOT NSOTED NSDEOT NSTODE
NSEDTO NSOTDE NSDETO NSTOED

NTSEOD NTESOD NTOESD NTDSEO
NTSEDO NTESDO NTOEDS NTDSOE
NTSODE NTEDOS NTOSDE NTDOSE
NTSDEO NTEDSO NTOSED NTDOES
NTSODE NTEOSD NTODSE NTDEOS
NTSDED NTEODS NTODES NTDESO

NDSTOE NDTSOE NDOTSE NDEOTS
NDSTEO NDTSEO NDOTES NDEOST
NDSEOT NDTEOS NDOEST NDESTO
NDSETO NDTESO NDOETS NDESOT
NDSOTE NDTOSE NDOSTE NDETOS
NDSOET NDTOES NDOSET NDETSO

TENDOS	TESNDO	TEDINO	TEODSN
TENOSD	TESNOD	TEDION	TEODNS
TENSDO	TESOND	TEDOSN	TEONDS
TENSOD	TESODN	TEDONS	TEONSD
TENODS	TESDON	TEDNSO	TEOSDN
TENOSD	TESDNO	TEDNOS	TEOSND

TSEDON	TSODEN	TINDOE	TSONOE
TSEDNO	TSODNE	TINDEO	TSDNED
TSENDO	TSONDE	TINEDO	TSDENO
TSENOD	TSONED	TINEOD	TSDEON
TSEOND	TSOEND	TINOED	TSDOEN
TSEODN	TSOEDN	TSNODE	TSDONE

TOSEND	TOEDSN	TONSED	TODESN
TOSEDN	TOEDNS	TONSDE	TODENS
TOSDEN	TOENSD	TONDSE	TODNES
TOSDNE	TOENDS	TONDES	TODNSE
TOSNED	TOESDN	TONEDS	TODSEN
TOSNDE	TOESND	TONESD	TODSNE

TNDEOS	TNSEDO	TNESDO	TNODSE
TNDESO	TNSEOD	TNESOD	TNODES
TNDSEO	TNSODE	TNEOSD	TNOSED
TNDSOE	TNSOED	TNEODS	TNOSDE
TNDOSE	TNSDOE	TNEDSO	TNOEDS
TNDOES	TNSDEO	TNEDOS	TNOESD

TDESON	TDSEON	TDNSEO	TDOSNE
TDESNO	TDSENO	TDNSOE	TDOSEN
TDEONS	TDSNEO	TDNOSE	TDOESN
TDEOSN	TDSNOE	TDNOES	TDOENS
TDENOS	TDSONE	TDNEOS	TDONES
TDENSO	TDSOEN	TDNESO	TDONSE

DOSTEN	DOTSEN	DOESTN	DONEST
DOSTNE	DOTSNE	DOESNT	DONETS
DOSNTE	DOTNES	DOENTS	DONTES
DOSNET	DOTNSE	DOENTS	DONTSE
DOSETN	DOTESN	DOETSN	DONSET
DOSENT	DOTENS	DOETNS	DONSTE

DSTOEN	DSOTEN	DSEOTN	DSNEOT
DSTONE	DSOTNE	DSEONT	DSNETO
DSTNOE	DSONET	DSENOT	DSNTOE
DSTNEO	DSONTE	DSENTO	DSNTEO
DSTENO	DSOETN	DSEINO	DSNOTE
DSTEON	DSOENT	DSETON	DSNOET

DNSTEO	DNTSEO	DNETSO	DNOETS
DNSTOE	DNTSOE	DNETOS	DNOEST
DNSIOTE	DNTOEJ	DNEOTS	DNOSTE
DNSOET	DNTOSE	DNEOTS	DNOSET
DNSEOT	DNTEOS	DNESTO	DNOTES
DNSETO	DNTESO	DNESOT	DNOTSE

DESTON	DETSON	DEOTSN	DENOTS
DESTNO	DETSNO	DEOTNS	DENOST
DESNOT	DETOSN	DEOSTN	DENSOT
DESNTO	DETONS	DEOSNT	DENSTO
DESONT	DETNOS	DEONTS	DENTSO
DESOTN	DETNSO	DEONST	DENTOS

DTSEON	DTESON	DTOESN	DTNOES
DTSENO	DTESNO	DTOENS	DTNOSE
DTSNEO	DTENOS	DTONSE	DTNEOS
DTSNOE	DTENSO	DTONES	DTNESO
DTSOEN	DTEOSN	DTOSEN	DTNSEO
DTSONE	DTEONS	DTOSNE	DTNSOE

Ostend, 2010, Aluminium/Acryl/Vinyl/Seekiefer
je 70 x 70 x 200 cm (zweiteilig)

S. 112, *Ostend* (Ausstellungsansicht), 2010

S. 113, *Night Star* (Detail), 2010, 82,5 x 70,5, Acryl/Leinen

Das Ding mit dem E, 2011
Aluminium/Acryl/Vinyl/Seekiefer
160 x 70 x 80 cm

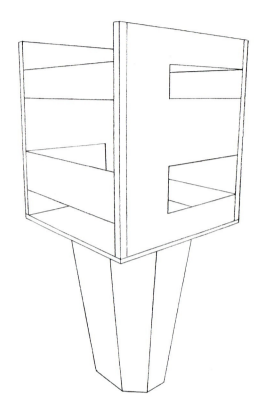

S. 116–119, *Das Ding mit dem E*, 2011
4C Print Collage, 60 x 50 cm

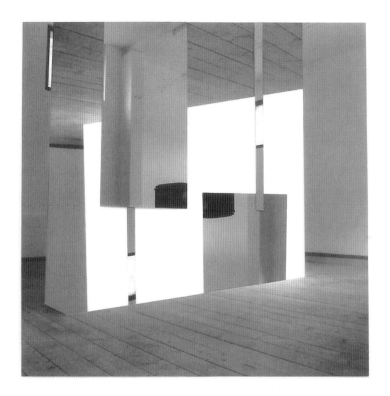

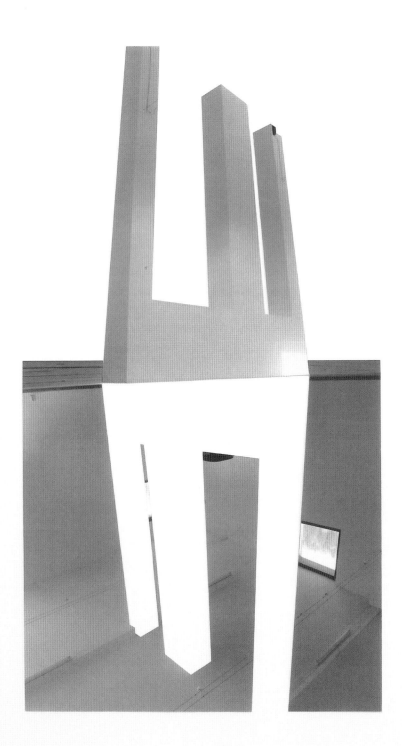

Dome, 2009
Acryl/Vinyl/Seekiefer
4 Elemente je 63 x 60 x 60 cm

Errata, 2011
Acryl/Vinyl/Seekiefer
27 x 25 x 1,8 cm

Autorin und Autoren

Thomas Ballhausen

(*1975 in Wien), Autor, Film- und Literaturwissenschaftler. Studium der Vergleichenden Literaturwissenschaft und der Deutschen Philologie an der Universität Wien. Wissenschaftlicher Mitarbeiter am Filmarchiv Austria, Lehrbeauftragter an der Universität Wien, Mitarbeiter zahlreicher internationaler Forschungsprojekte. Literarische, essayistische und wissenschaftliche Publikationen. Mehrere selbstständige Veröffentlichungen, u.a.: *Delirium und Ekstase. Die Aktualität des Monströsen* (Wien, 2008) und *Bewegungsmelder* (Innsbruck, 2010).

Matthias Boeckl

lehrt Geschichte und Theorie der Architektur an der Universität für angewandte Kunst Wien. Seit 1999 ist er Chefredakteur der zweisprachig erscheinenden, internationalen Fachzeitschrift *architektur.aktuell*. Er ist Autor zahlreicher Aufsätze und Bücher und ist als Ausstellungskurator zu Themen der modernen und zeitgenössischen Kunst und Architektur tätig.

Martin Engler

(*1968 Freiburg) studierte Kunstgeschichte, Germanistik und Rechtswissenschaften in Freiburg und Florenz. Von 1997-2005 freier Kurator und Kunstkritiker (u.a. für FAZ., Die Zeit, NZZ, Kunstbulletin) 1998-2002 Akademiedozent mit Schwerpunkt Gegenwartskunst. 2002-2008 Kurator am Kunstverein Hannover. Seit 2008 Kurator und Sammlungsleiter für Kunst nach 1945 am Städel Museum Frankfurt/Main.

Jan Mokre

Kartenhistoriker und Bibliothekar, wurde 1961 in Berlin geboren und lebt seit 1984 in Wien. Er studierte an der Universität Wien Neue Geschichte und spezialisierte sich auf Kartographiegeschichte, Entdeckungsgeschichte und auf die Geschichte außereuropäischer Völker. 2002 wurde er zum Direktor der Kartensammlung und des Globenmuseums der ÖNB ernannt. Er ist Generalsekretär der Internationalen Coronelli-Gesellschaft für Globenkunde. Mokre veröffentlichte zahlreiche Aufsätze zur Karten- und Globengeschichte sowie Rezensionen in wissenschaftlichen Fachzeitschriften.

Annette Südbeck

ist Kuratorin an der Secession, Wien, wo sie in jüngster Zeit u.a. Austellungen mit Michael Snow, Stephen Prina, Manfred Pernice und Lara Almarcegui erarbeitete. 2011 veröffentlichte sie ihre Dissertation *Eine andere Art zu zeichnen. Die Wandzeichnung bei Sol LeWitt, Hilka Nordhausen und David Tremlett*.

Authors

Thomas Ballhausen

(*1975 in Vienna), author, film and literary scholar. Studied Comparative Literature and German philology at the Unvresity of Vienna. Member of research staff at the Filmarchiv Austra, lecturer at the University of Vienna. Has collaborated in a number of international research projects. Literary texts, essays and scholarly publications. A number of books published, among them: *Delirium und Ekstase. Die Aktualität des Monströsen* (Vienna, 2008) and *Bewegungsmelder* (Innsbruck, 2010).

Matthias Boeckl

teaches history and theory of architecture at the Univresity of Applied Arts in Vienna. Since 1999 he is editor-in-chief of the bilingual international journal architektur.aktuell. He is the author of numerous essays and books and has worked as exhibition curaturs on themes of modern and contempoary art and architecture.

Martin Engler

(*1968 Freiburg) studied art history, German literature and philology, and law in Freiburg and Florence. From 1997 to 2005 free-lance curator and art critic (FAZ, Die Zeit, NZZ, Kunstbulletin, among others) 1998-2002 instructor at the Art Academy with a focus on contemporary art. 2002-2008 curator at Kunstverein Hannover. Since 2008 curator and head of post-1945 art collection at Städel Museum Frankfurt/Main.

Jan Mokre

map historian and librarian, born 1961 in Berlin and lives in Vienna since 1984. He studied modern history at the University of Vienna and specialized in cartographic history, history of discovery and the history of non-European peoples. In 2002 he was appointed director of the Map Collection and Globe Museum of the Austrian Nat. Library. He is secretary general of the international Coronelli Society for Globe Studies. Mokre has published numerous essays on map and globe history as well as reviews in scholarly journals.

Annette Südbeck

is a curator at the Secession in Vienna, where she has most recently organized solo exhibitions with Michael Snow, Stephen Prina, Manfred Pernice, and Lara Almarcegui. In 2011 she published her dissertation on wall drawings, *Eine andere Art zu zeichnen. Die Wandzeichnung bei Sol LeWitt, Hilka Nordhausen und David Tremlett*.

Eric Kressnig

1973   geboren in Klagenfurt
1996–2001   Studium der Malerei und Grafik
            Akademie der Bildenden Künste, Wien

PREISE STIPENDIEN

2011	Rudolf Hradil Stipendium, Salzburg
2010	Atelierstipendium der Stadt Wien in Frankfurt am Main
2008	Staatsstipendium für Bildende Kunst
2007	Parisstipendium des Landes Kärnten
2002	CA-Kunstpreis, Kärnten
2001	Stipendium der Sussmann Stiftung
2001	Meisterklassenpreis Akademie der Bildenden Künste, Wien

EINZELAUSSTELLUNGEN

2012	Jesuitenfoyer, Wien
	rittergallery, Klagenfurt
2007	adapted land, Galerie Edition Stalzer, Wien □
2006	different levels of adapted land, habres+partner, Wien □
	react view, splitter art, Wien □
2005	we are arena, white8 Galerie, Villach □
2004	perspective of the veranda, habres+partner, Wien
2003	Alte Schmiede, Wien
2002	Widmanneum, Villach

GRUPPENAUSSTELLUNGEN (Auswahl)

2012	Realität und Abstraktion – Konkrete und reduktive Tendenzen ab 1980, Museum Liaunig, Neuhaus/Suha +
2011	Streng Geometrisch, MMKK, Klagenfurt + □
	Konstrukt und Poesie, mit Bella Ban, [kunstwerk] krastal +
2010	Artist in Residence Jahresausstellung, atelierfrankfurt, Frankfurt am Main +
	tooltime, flat1, Wien
	transform2, Kunstverein Kärnten, Klagenfurt
	multiple choice, Galerie Edition Stalzer, Wien □
2009	Raumordnungen, Bäckerstraße 4 Plattform für aktuelle Kunst, Wien
	augmented, Galerie Strickner, Wien
	Zeichen.Struktur.Reduktion. Sammlung Urban, Waidhofen/Ybbs
	Sommerhoch, mit Ferdinand Penker, rittergallery, Klagenfurt
	Socha A Objekt XIV., Bratislava +
2008	Positionen Kressnig Penker Taupe, rittergallery, Klagenfurt
	K08 Emanzipation und Konfrontation – Kunst aus Kärnten von 1945 bis heute, Werner Berg Museum, Bleiburg +
	Prints for New York, LeRoy Neiman Center, Columbia University, New York +
2007	views from abroad, mit Regina Zachhalmel SWINGR, Wien □
	Blickwechsel No 3, MMKK, Klagenfurt +
	Cité Internationale des Arts Paris
	Andreas Stalzer 20 Jahre Werkstatt für Kunstsiebdruck, NÖ-Dokumentationszentrum für Moderne Kunst, St.Pölten
	Walter Koschatzky Kunstpreis-Ausstellung, MUMOK, Wien
2006	radiostation, Projektraum Kunstraum, Innsbruck + □
	2,91, mit Robert Kummer, rittergallery, Klagenfurt
	crossover, Koroska, Galerija, Slovenj Gradec, Slowenien +
	dejavu, Stadtgalerie Klagenfurt +
	spring, Galerie 3, Klagenfurt
2005	Stripes-Lines-Colors, Galerie Wolfgang Exner, Wien
	Walter Koschatzky Kunstpreis-Ausstellung, MUMOK, Wien
2004	white8 Galerie, Villach
2003	Galerie 3, Klagenfurt
	Atelier Berndt, mit Manuel Knapp, Wolfsberg
	area 53, mit Philip Haselwandter, Wien
2002	Überblick, Galerie Exner, Wien
	Welcome, Künstlerhaus Klagenfurt □
	Vel Satis Award, Kunst Wien +
2001	Junge Figuren, Galerie 422, Gmunden
	Hommage a Louise Bourgeois, Kupferstichkabinett, Wien +
	2.Stock, Wien □
	Coming out – Analyse, Künstlerhaus, Klagenfurt +
1999	young line 3rd, Galerie Station 3, Wien
1998	Junge Kunst vom Stein, Kupferstichkabinett, Wien +
	academies-spices-diversities, Semperdepot, Wien

\+ Katalog
□ sitespecific work

Besonderen Dank an:

Walter Fußeis
Christian Slugovc
Andreas Stalzer

Beilage: Poster, *Case Studies – For an unknown space nearby*, 78 x 49 cm

Zu diesem Buch erscheint eine signierte und nummerierte Vorzugsausgabe bei rittergallery, Klagenfurt.

Impressum:

ISBN: 978-3-85415-486-0

© 2012 Eric Kressnig, VBK-Wien, Ritter Verlag
sowie bei den einzelnen Autoren.

Übersetzung: Camilla Nielsen

Lektorat: Georg Mitsche

Fotos: Mark Duran, S. 25, 30/31, 51, 70–72, 75, 88
Ferdinand Neumüller, S. 42, 43
WMWP Rechtsanwälte, S.19
Sammlung Liaunig, S. 21–23
Regina Zachhalmel, S. 4
alle weiteren Fotos, Eric Kressnig

Bildbearbeitung: Mark Duran

Design: Eric Kressnig / Mark Duran / Regina Zachhalmel

Herstellung: Ritter Klagenfurt

www.ritterbooks.com

www.rittergallery.com

www.kressnig.com

Mit freundlicher Unterstützung: